Diary of a Lesbian Housewyfe

Delightful Stories, Yummy Recipes & Gay Household Hints

LA Bourgeois

LuckyChix Press

CONTENTS

·♥· ♥· ♥·♥· ♥·

IN THE BEGINNING

B ack in 1990, I met my future wyfe.

First day of acting class at 9am on a Monday morning. I sat on the floor, hanging on my boyfriend, waiting for the teacher to walk into the studio.

My acting teacher entered the room with a new friend in tow, laughing as she put down her things. The new friend was Stephanie, a tall, muscular woman with long, curly red-blonde hair. As soon as I saw her, my breath caught in my chest and a voice, as clear as any voice I've ever heard in my ears, rang through my brain.

"This is the person you will spend the rest of your life with."

Well, no. No. Of course not. The person I was going to spend the rest of my life with was sitting beside me. And was a man.

Fast forward two and a half years. The boyfriend (then fiancee, then nothing) was gone and Stephanie and I were living together.

As I set up my new household, my mother signed me up for a subscription to *Taste of Home* magazine.

The "community cookbook" feel of *Taste of Home* charmed and intrigued me, and their "When I Was A Young Housewife" column particularly pulled me in. These stories made me laugh and feel so superior to the hapless young ladies figuring out how ingredients work together or filling their homes with smoke. One of my favorites was about a woman who knew she should put "spice" in spaghetti sauce, so she added tons of cinnamon to the sauce. After staring at her husband dutifully choking down this odd concoction, she finally took a bite and knew how much he loved her as she gagged.

In our first year of living together, my darling wyfe gave me the gift of a year off. She worked while I hung out at home and housewifed around.

Perhaps I was the first lesbian housewife? Or was it you?

One way or the other, these are my tales of my twenties and thirties as a modern housewife. By which I mean, a woman who often works outside the house, but still takes on the majority of the household duties.

So, without delay...

When I was a Young (and not-so-young) Housewyfe, this is what transpired.

·♥·♥·♥·♥·♥·

THE BASIC MODEL

H ello.

My name is LA Bourgeois.

I am a Lesbian Housewyfe.

I don't know if there is a twelve-step program for this and, if there was, I don't know if I would go.

Or, perhaps, I just created one.

I hope not.

Anyway, for those of you who don't know what a Lesbian Housewyfe is, I am a very select group. I like to call myself the "millenium's June Cleaver." For now I remain alone in embracing that faux Fifties feminine lifestyle, but perhaps, someday, others will come out of that broom closet and join me in the joyous life of gardening, household duties, and interior design.

Let me remind you of the ever famous, ever young, ever timely television series "Leave it to Beaver." June was the Beaver's mom. She wore pearls to wash the dishes and never got that wet line of soapy water across her belly. She was the perfect hostess. Her hair, always neatly coiffed, never moved. She was pristine and perfect even when she camped.

Of course, now she is camp.

The important part of this comparison is that June stayed home and so do I. Ward supported the whole family in a monetary fashion while June supported the family by taking care of their huge suburban household and managing somehow to feed three men and herself with wonderful hearty meals every evening. Without the help of a maid.

June never drank on television, but I know she would have in real life. I bet we could document this. She was a typical Fifties housewife.

June is now held up as a model for the rest of us as the country follows its mistaken struggle to find those more innocent times of the Fifties.

(Does anyone remember "Rebel Without a Cause?")

I am the new June. I have rejected the idea of a conventional household. I only wear pearls when I'm actually leaving the house, I step away from the sink with watery clothes, and my hair is never fixed beyond a simple ponytail. I will never go camping even though it violates Lesbian Law #4: "I embrace and rejoice in every small chance to revel in Mother Nature even if it means going without showers and pooping in a hole in the woods."

My family is made up of myself and my spouse. No children yet -- unless you include my mother-in-law, two cats, one dog, and the dog we babysit every day. And her owner. And my mother-in-law's boyfriend. And several of our friends who seem to live at our house. And this one college student who lived in our basement for a couple of years and now gives us Mother's Day cards.

But no presents. This is what comes from skipping that formal marriage thing!

But I digress...

My partner supports me for the most part, while I work out of the house. Perhaps a more accurate person would say that I work in the house.

Now, I say I am a computer consultant. I say I am a writer. I say I am an actress.

I am not a liar. I just don't have enough time in the day. Do you know how much time it takes to keep up a house? Perfectly? Do you know how much time I spend baking fresh bread for my household? Do you know how much time I spend gardening so we can have fresh vegetables on the table? Do you know how little time it takes them to eat all of these wonderful things? Do you know that I managed to kill a zucchini in Colorado where they grow like weeds?

Never you mind that last part.

My point is that I do tend to put the needs of others before my own. Or is that my own needs before others? Cloudiness sets in when one begins to enjoy cleaning toilets. My boundaries have become blurred. I mean to take that job, memorize that monologue, get started on that book idea. I just don't get around to it.

Suddenly, I am my mother. Or grandmother. Sometimes this thing skips a generation. Mom is actually a career person, breaking boundaries as a preacher, although I see the seeds of housewifery in her. Something must have sprung from that.

I have begun to value the importance of a clean house, fresh food, and new appliances. Buying a new dryer, a new blender, a new lawn mower sends me into ecstasy.

In fact, we just bought the greatest lawn mower of all: mulching, cordless and electric. It's convenient and yet it recycles. Lesbian Law #2: "Reduce, Reuse, Recycle."

I am a Lesbian Housewyfe. I am a June. I feel a strange rush of sexual excitement when I find a really good sale on tuna fish at Safeway that wasn't advertised. Albacore only, of course. Lesbian Law #17: "Never do anything that endangers a dolphin."

Ah yes, you may say, surely she must know the traditional role of the lesbian is a radical feminist one. What is she doing spreading this ugly "lesbian housewyfe" rumor? My only reply is Lesbian Law #1: "Never underestimate the power of a Lesbian Housewyfe."

No one I live with does.

WORLD FAMOUS TUNA CASSEROLE

My Daddy named this recipe. I have found that even people who hate tuna like this casserole. I think that may be because I smash and smash and smash the tuna into little itty-bitty bits. Making this casserole is worth at least an hour with the therapist working on your anger issues.

1 1 lb. bag of uncooked Wide Egg Noodles

2 T. butter

1 small onion, chopped into 1/4" pieces

2 ribs celery, chopped into 1/4" pieces

1 10 1/2 ounce can of Cream of Mushroom Soup

1 6 ounce can of Tuna Fish

1 - 1 1/2 t. Spike (or other house seasoning you may have around)

3/4 can (use the same can as the Cream of Mushroom Soup) Whole Milk

1 generous splash white wine

1 1/2 cups grated Monterey Jack Cheese

1 small can french-fried onions

Follow the directions on the side of the bag to cook egg noodles. While the noodles are cooking, preheat the oven to 350 degrees and drain your can of tuna fish.

Melt the butter over medium heat in your cast iron skillet and saute the onion and celery until the onion is translucent.

Smash up the tuna and combine it with the cream of mushroom soup, milk, wine and spike in a big bowl (you're going to add the noodles to it). Add the sauteed onion and celery to the tuna mixture and combine well.

Taste, taste, taste! If you need extra seasoning, add it. Remember that the noodles will take up some of your salt, so this mixture should taste a little salty.

When the noodles are done to your satisfaction (I like them al dente), drain them and combine with the tuna mixture.

Pour that mixture into a greased 9″x13″ pan and spread grated cheese and french-fried onions over the top of the casserole.

Bake for 1/2 hour or until heated through with lovely touches of golden brown on top.

Mmmmmmm....pretty.

I serve this casserole in generous pasta bowls with fresh green beans and carrot salad (see recipe below).

CARROT SALAD

My sweet honey-bunny and I struggled to find a name for this satisfying salad before quietly settling on the above.

1 bag of baby carrots

Open bag of carrots. Take out one handful and place on each plate. Serve.

·♥·♥·♥·♥·♥·

A Short Explanation of Husbynds & Wyves

O ne day this past summer, I sat in a friend's home watching my lovely wyfe and our lovely hostesses bustle about the kitchen and make dinner.

It is not often that the Lesbian Housewyfe gets a break and this one was blissful! I reclined on a couch in the living area, read magazines and drank a beer. Mmmmm. I went through my friend's extensive collection of publications one by one until I reached this one particular gay magazine with Greg Louganis on the cover. Intrigued by the promise of an excerpt, I opened and started flipping.

Somehow I landed on an article expressing the general frustration of the homosexual community over the lack of a label for our "life partners." Reading that article, I realized my mission. This idea could have some merit, I thought. Now for the acid test.

I bounded into the kitchen area and exclaimed, "I have the answer!"

All regarded me with suspicion. Only my sweet wyfe was brave enough to venture. "LA.... What exactly is it the answer to?"

"The gay spousal label problem!" I stated proudly.

"Oh." Everyone relaxed and went back to their duties. As I thought they were rather dismissive, I chose not to reveal until they asked.

Steph chopped up a cucumber.

I will not tell, I will not tell, I thought over and over.

Pasta dropped into boiling water.

I bit my lips together.

Sauce dripped down the side of a jar.

"Well, since you asked...."

No one responded.

"Wyfe-with-a-y and husbynd-with-a-y!"

"Uh-huh." A voice from the kitchen encouraged.

I barged on. "You see, I got the idea from womyn-with-a-y. I was just reading this article about the whole problem and this lady seems so emphatic that none of the words we are using are specific or emotional enough. What is the answer? What words could we use to signify the warm fuzzy aspects of our relationship and still show the formality of our commitment? What words could we use to emphasize the nontraditional formation of our relationships? What words can we use to show our true and complete partnerships? Well, what word best describes the formal familial status of Stephanie in my life? My answer to that question is that she is my wyfe. You like that label, don't you honey?"

She nodded (in recognition of Lesbian Law #11: Value and treasure every remark your partner utters (serious or silly) and back her up, if need be) and I continued.

"So you see, since the words husband and wife are so widely recognized, then it follows that husbynd-with-a-y and wyfe-with-a-y would retain the easy recognition and carry the emotional and formal status of this relationship without ambiguity. At the same time, these words (rather aptly, I think) point out the nontraditional form of the relationship through the spelling and non-gender-specific use."

My friend's lover piped up, "So I can be a husbynd?"

"Yes!" I exclaimed, delighted that she grasped the concept so quickly. I must be making sense, I thought, and started doing cheers in my head.

"Does that mean I have to be the wyfe?" My forty-five year old radical lesbian friend asked defensively.

The screaming fans fell silent.

Whatever, I thought, and placed special emphasis on that second syllable so as to emulate that ever-so-ubiquitous junior high brush-off. I took a deep cleansing breath. "No. You can both be husbynds or both wyves or one be a wyfe and one a husbynd. It's more personal preference than anything else and, frankly (or janely), it could change from day to day."

"Hmmm." She said and I could tell the idea appealed to her. Yes! I thought and the fans began to cheer once again.

Then the questions began to fly.

"Can a wyfe mow the grass?"

"Every day."

"Can a husbynd cook?"

"Don't marry 'em if they can't"

"What about gardening?"

"Either or both as far as I'm concerned."

"Cleaning."

"You could be a house husbynd."

"Can a housewyfe have a job?"

A long silent stare was my only reply.

My forty-five year old radical lesbian friend giggled.

She actually giggled.

"Don't be a goober," I replied. "I think it's basically whatever you feel more comfortable with. Do you feel like a husbynd or a wyfe?"

"Husbynd."

"Well, that's that then, isn't it." I said. Now that I look back at the incident, I might have been a bit snippy because my forty-five year old radical lesbian friend looked sharply through astonished eyes and I knew I was in it now. I steeled myself for the storm that can be created by a womyn-with-a-y who has seen first-handboth the oppression of the patriarchy and the acceptance of the Michigan Womyn's Festival. She lived through Stonewall. She worked in a lesbian-owned womyn's bookstore. She's done radical lesbian guerrilla theatre. She's held pot-lucks.

I had broken Lesbian Law #24: Never, ever cross a crone.

I was so in trouble.

My heart beat faster.

Her laughter escaped in a huge bark followed by a trail of giggles from everyone.

I almost fainted.

"Well," I breathed a silent sigh of relief and swallowed, "isn't this a great idea?"

"I think," my forty-five year old radical lesbian friend replied, "this idea could have some merit."

And I wisely allowed the conversation to deteriorate into gossip about old friends and cooking instructions.

But I smiled knowingly for the rest of the evening because I know Lesbian Law #1: Never Underestimate the Power of a Lesbian Housewyfe.

This idea could have some merit.

·♥·♥·♥·♥·♥·

HINTS FOR A HAPPY MARRIAGE

L ots of my friends ask me, "How can I have a wonderful and happy marriage just like you, LA?"

They call me LA because they don't know me as Mrs. Lesbian Housewyfe and also because that is actually my name.

"LA," they say, "Reveal your secrets."

I say, "Unconditional love and communication.'"

And they say, "No, really."

Well, here it really is.

How can you have a happy marriage just like me?

You can't.

Well, you could, I suppose, but first you would have to steal away my little honey bunny and that, I understand from her vehement protestations as she leans over my shoulder to participate in that little known party game "back-seat writing," would be pretty much impossible. So I guess you'll need to find your own person to keep you.

Pick someone you really like as well as love and who loves you back in just the same way. If you can't find someone like that, pick someone wealthy. Really, the most important part of this decision is just to make a decision.

Too many times I find my poor bumbling friends running frantically down that road of life tripping and falling into the roses when they turn their heads to get a mere glance of the beauty instead of just taking some time out.

NEWSFLASH--> All that gets you is a butt full of thorns.

If you were to actually stop, you might find someone else taking a whiff of that sweet perfume. Now, this is a person to take a little walk with.

Those people that you bump against accidentally and sprint with for a ways-well, let's just say, one will become fatigued quickly if one exercises that hard.

Problems can also arise when people find someone to walk with and, while they innocently stroll along together holding hands and enjoying the view, someone runs by. That running looks exciting and they've forgotton how tiring it is. You know you're in trouble when you're still enjoying the walk and your partner starts to jog. You'll be okay if you can keep up or if they slow down soon, but let it go if they sprint ahead and out of view.

The factor which makes the difference is when two people (both partners) choose to walk and jog and run down the entire path together, keeping stride or at least waiting at the benches for each other.

So you can see that the most important and primary step to the happy marriage is the decision to be with each other forever.

After that, it's just a matter of formula and an Indy pace car.

Or perhaps a cosmic stop watch.

Now, here are three recipes for a happy marriage.

1. THE INTENSE RELATIONSHIP

Take one heavy cast iron frying pan.

Use liberally.

Generally, this classic recipe works mainly on a traditional caveman level. The bonks on the head keep your mate in line through continual slight unconsciousness and the food keeps her coming back for more. Considered very efficient, this recipe does tend to violate Lesbian Law #3: "Never smack your mate or current lover or even cheap one night stand up the side of the head or anywhere else unless they ask you to."

One can generally assume your mate doesn't want to be knocked around like this on a long-term basis, so it tends to lead to a short, intense experience. Of course, one might be wrong.

2. The Fat and Happy Relationship

Take 3 parts good cooking

2 parts excellent gardening

1 part great sex

A dash of hedonism

Mix all ingredients together vigorously. Add extra hedonism to taste.

Tending to excess in all, this recipe guarantees that one won't walk away with a trim waistline, but it is a pleasant experience to say the least. However, as soon as any of these ingredients spoil, the end product becomes rancid.

3. The Final and Forever Recipe

Equal parts of Unconditional Love

Complete Expression

"Insta-truth"

Flexibility for Change in both partners

Good Listening Skills

Mix together gently and use thoroughly.

This recipe works well on a continuing basis. Life isn't quite so exciting at times, but the trade-off of extra energy for your own stuff makes the difference. Remember also that the romps behind the rose-bushes don't have to end just because you've been together for two weeks.

Now, one of the ingredients in this recipe defies immediate defini-tion. That is "Insta-truth," also known as "telling the truth as quickly as possible." Just as effective as a good sex toy, this ingredient will keep your relationship well lubricated and moving easily through every facet of your life, not just the bedroom (although it won't hurt there).

My partner and I use a healthy combination of the second two. While I highly recommend this amalgamation to everyone, I know some of us haven't moved past the first recipe.

Move on, baby. Life is too short for one more bad lay... I mean, day.

For those of you who don't believe me anyway (and I know you're out there), just remember Lesbian Law #1: "Never underestimate the power of a Lesbian Housewyfe."

I'm a happy little camper.

How to Season Your Cast Iron Skillet

Well, first you have to obtain a cast iron skillet. You could purchase an old one at a garage sale, or find one on the internet, or steal that one from your mother's house. Personally, I went to a big box department store and bought an unseasoned one straight off the shelf. No big personal drama, except when I got home and realized that this one was gray and not black like my Mother's. I called her immediately and asked why. She told me I had to season it.

Season? No one mentioned this to me! Sure, there were some sort of instructions on the back of the label, but who doesn't know how to use a pan. I mean, "Set on stove. Apply heat. Cook food." Duh! I threw those instructions away immediately without even reading them.

Now, of course, I dug through the trash to find that bit of paper. Emerging triumphant from the garbage can, I read the label carefully.

Before seasoning, scrub the pan with hot water, dish soap, and a scouring pad to remove wax. To season, coat the pan with shortening and heat for an hour in a 500 degree oven. Allow to cool completely.

And that was it. I wasn't sure what wax they meant, but I followed the directions and ended up with a house that smelled suspiciously of hot pan burning on top of the stove.

Probably because a hot pan was burning inside the oven.

I allowed the skillet to cool until I could touch it.

Still gray.

I called my mother.

"Honey, eventually the pan will turn black. For now, make sure not to clean it with dishwashing soap; just hot water and elbow grease.

Maybe use some salt if you need to scour it, but otherwise just hot water. Heat it on the stove to dry and you'll be all set."

To this suggestion, my sweet honey-bunny added that her mother had always swirled a light coating of vegetable oil over the hot cast iron skillet with a paper towel.

I began my journey with my skillet, cooking and cleaning and seasoning. In just a few uses, the surface began to darken. A couple of months later, the slick black surface of the seasoned skillet shone.

If the pan needs to be scoured, pour a generous layer of salt in after you've done your initial scrub and allow it to marinate for a few minutes. Then, use your wet sponge to scrub out the pan. The stuck-on detritus will come right off, most times with little effort.

As my cast iron continued its journey, a buildup of charred carbon coated the outside of the pan. I never minded very much, but if you want to get rid of that build-up (either because you have inherited the pan or just want it gone after many years of usage), I've found suggestions online ranging from a simple baking soda solution to using a wire brush attached to a drill.

Well meaning folks managed to wash the sucker with dishwashing soap several times which meant an extra coating of oil after cleaning for about a month to regain the almost nonstick quality of a well-seasoned cast iron skillet.

I can honestly say that I use this skillet almost every day, that nothing cooks or bakes with the precision and heat of the pan, and that there is nothing so useful as a good cast iron skillet.

After all, what other object in your house could you use as a weapon?

Maybe you shouldn't answer that.

·♥·♥·♥·♥·♥·

SHE'S A WORKING GIRL

By now, I'm sure you're thinking, "Well, that little Lesbian Housewyfe is just a Generation X slacker who's trying to cover up her lack of a job by turning her life into a series of anecdotes."

Not quite, Charlie.

I don't just stay at home even though that is what a housewyfe does. You know I live to scrub toilets and gently hand-wash delicates but the life of a modern housewyfe is complicated. The modern "June Cleaver" is more likely to be an ad executive than a full-time gardening earth momma.

It has become essential to be, I hate to say it, employed in some way.

I'm afraid that in these days where both partners in a marriage must work, it is pretty much impossible for one to stay at home full-time—a sad subject for the lovely Lesbian Housewyfe. I get choked up just thinking about it.

A forlorn howl in the night from a domesticated wolf (or a "housewyfe who runs with the wolves") seems to say, "Why must this be?" Tears form as it wails loudly through the night.

Neighbors throw old balled up socks at it.

Therefore, to keep the noise down, I have a little business on the side.

Not that kind of business!

I'm a computer consultant.

I do enough cleaning in my own home. No need to cast my cleaning pearls before swine.

Actually, computer consultant might be a bit restrictive in the description of what I do. I'm an all around kind of cybergal in terms of sitting in front of a glowing box all day. Generally, I take odd jobs which I then group together under the general category of "computer consulting."

The operative word here is odd. A very special piece of advice from the Lesbian Housewyfe: NEVER answer a want ad asking for an "open-minded" typist. I ended up typing porn for a rich short man who had no concept of anatomy. The money was good but it was almost painful to type these bizarre female wrestling pseudolesbian sex scenes. The laughter, I hate to say, abounded as I realized he had all the wrong names attached to the wrong parts and most of the positions were quite impossible (water up your nose, etc.). The dream ended when he asked me if I had any friends who would like to stage a little match for him. I had to say, "I'm a typist, not a pimp."

The relationship ended abruptly.

Even stranger, I sometimes, on the occasion, the very slim and far between occasion, am a temporary.

Just for myself though; I'm not a whore either.

Now, what, you may ask, is strange about this?

What is not strange about temping?

You go to someone else's workplace that they hate so much they got totally sick just thinking about going in this morning and you fill in for them. Usually with only a half-hour notice.

Temporaries are the substitute teachers of the business world. After a few spitballs in the back of the head, you start to wonder who thought this up. I mean, who would do this?

Actually, apparently I would and a huge industry has built itself around this need, but it's still odd. I can do it though. I do type very well.

To my parent's financial dismay, I am college educated and heard that same speech we all heard from our guidance counselor in high school.

"You, [insert your name here], are planning to go to college?"

A brave "Yes." from you.

"You need to know how to type for college."

A blank look from you. "Really?"

"You get better grades if you type your papers and most professors make you do it anyway. Look, it fits into your schedule right here in place of sex education (or art or theater or study hall)."

"But...." You begin to pull your class schedule slowly from their grasp.

Sharp look from the guidance counselor as they forcefully pen in the change on your class schedule.

End of discussion.

So I can type.

My typing skills expanded quickly once I got to college to include general wordprocessing. In my household, I use the computer to do the books and to keep track of my household duties. In your workplace, I work wonders with my little typing fingers.

Thank God for my high school counselor who kept me out of Coach's sex-ed class. That could have been ugly!

Plus, if things ever get too rough, I can always sell Amway.

"NO!!!!" The voices from beyond are screaming. "Not Amway! You are our hero, our Earth Mother, our Goddess!!! You can't be an Amway distributor! Our dreams are destroyed. Our perfect vision of housewifehood desecrated!" On and on they despair through the night, for yes, I am on that fateful Amway list.

So much for quiet nights in my neighborhood.

Fortunately, being the really grotesquely horrible salesperson that I am, I will probably never obtain the status which my cousin, my sponsor, wishes. Of course, the family roped me into this. Lesbian Law #15: Support your family in all they do, even if it's Amway. I have yet to sell a single product to anyone but myself. So, the larger world can rest easy, for the lovely Lesbian Housewyfe is also a horrible black hole in the land of multilevel marketing.

This is not really a viable option. I just keep it in mind in case I'm ever that desperate.

So you can see, I am perfectly willing to jump in when the times get a bit threatening financially. Luckily, I am able to completely and freely choose my life as the Lovely Lesbian Housewyfe. I am not a Generation X slacker. And I hate the term—who the hell thought up Generation X anyway? Some ad geek.

I know these things. My parents sent me to college.

They understand Lesbian Law #1: Never underestimate the power of a Lesbian Housewyfe.

Anyone need any Amway?

***Quick note to anyone born after 1975: People used to teach typing in high school before computers became ubiquitous. I learned to touch-type in 1985 on an IBM Selectric typewriter. These days, you can find typewriters in museums, specialized repair shops, and the homes of avid collectors and authors. Want to see a picture? Look it up on the Google, you young scamp!*

MOSTLY HANDS OFF PASTA

After I've battled the workplace all day, I can't even think about dinner. My sweet honey-bunny lands in the same boat, so I've come up with this easy solution to coast through the first hour of the evening. It's a nice change up from sloshing a jar of tomato sauce into a pan. Plus, decompressing from the day by doing a little smashing of a clove of garlic never hurt anyone, and may have prevented harm from coming to someone else.

4-6 slices bacon, chopped into 1/2" slices

1 lb. Asparagus or broccoli, chopped into 1" lengths or small florets

3 cloves garlic, smashed

2 T. olive oil, divided

1/4 c. chopped walnuts

1/2 lb linguine

1/2 c. grated asiago or parmesan, plus extra for serving

Preheat the oven to 425 degrees. Combine bacon, asparagus or broccoli, garlic and olive oil in a 8"x8" square pan and put in the oven. Stir occasionally until the bacon is almost done, about 20 minutes.

Meanwhile, bring a pot of water to boil on the stove and add your pasta. Cook to your preferred stage of doneness. I like mine just past *al dente*. Drain the pasta, reserving a little water if you like. Add the pasta back to your pan.

When the bacon is almost done, add the walnuts and stir them in. They will toast lightly during this time.

When the bacon is crispy, pull the pan from the oven and add the contents to the pasta. Toss it with another tablespoon of the olive oil.

Then add your 1/2 cup of grated cheese and toss again to blend.

Transfer to serving bowls and garnish with additional cheese. Serve immediately.

THE SALAD

This salad has become our supper staple. We eat it almost every night, and the timing always turns out well since you can leave it assembled but untossed for as long as a few hours.

1 clove garlic
pinch salt
1/4 c. rice wine vinegar
1/4 t. Dijon mustard
1/2 c. olive oil
1/2 avocado, chopped into 1/2" slices
1/4 cucumber, seeded and chopped into 1/4" pieces
8 cherry tomatoes, quartered
4 cups mixed greens

Mash the garlic and salt into a paste in a mortar and pestle. Add the vinegar and mush and stir it up a little more. Transfer the mixture into your salad bowl. Whisk in the mustard and then slowly add the olive oil, whisking the entire time to meld the mixture into a slightly thick emulsion. You know, the way salad dressing looks.

Add your avocado, cucumber and tomatoes to the dressing and toss them to coat. Then, top with the greens. This salad can be held like this for several hours. About five minutes before you are ready to serve, toss the salad well, making sure to coat all of the greens with the dressing. We eat our salad last, so I always serve it in the same bowl or plate as the rest of the dinner.

My sweet honey-bunny gets a good head start on cleanup by licking the serving spoons clean.

·❤ · ❤ · ❤ · ❤ · ❤ ·

TIPS ON COMING OUT

F or those of you who don't know, the LGBTQIA+ community
(See Lesbian Law #28: "Never, ever leave anyone out, no matter
how difficult it is to say.") celebrates October eleventh as Coming Out
Day, a lovely holiday complete with streamers and sparklers.

Okay, maybe more drama than actual sparklers, but as the lovely,
and perhaps only, Lesbian Housewyfe, I feel the need to make my two
cent deposit into your life on this very special day. A common problem
among those of us who have not even dusted our closet yet is how to
come out.

Now, I have come out to many of my family members except for
the eldest ones. My grandfather does have that heart condition and my
mother begged pathetically for me to spare her parents. Also, I believe
my grandfather, who is practically deaf along with being on just this
side of a coronary, wouldn't actually hear me and my grandmother,
who is periodically not in this dimension, wouldn't remember but
Mother is firm on this point and I am willing to give in to her demands.
I mean, who wants to be the big dork who killed her own grandparents
by coming out?

That's not a good way to make an impression.

To get back to our subject, the common problem is not whether
or not to come out. Every homosexual knows they need to come

out to combat the stereotypes of the lisping momma's boy and the flannel-lined androgyne.

Don't you hate those people who are all like "You must COME OUT!!" and then they aren't out to any of their family or straight friends? Or how about the ones who are out to everyone and every time they come out to someone it's an entire event and you are regaled with the story of the time they scolded the grocery bagger for making a homophobic remark in the middle of the Safeway parking lot?

I hate that. Their methods just don't work. They have no practical social skills. They expect you to just walk up to your boss one day and say, "Hey! I'm a big dyke!"

And your boss replies, "What's your name again?"

Well, here are some practical and time honored methods for coming out.

People you don't know are a piece of cake. When you eventually get around to the subject of your honey-bunny, you simply tell them. Much easier than telling Mom and Dad, who really should have known already. At least, that's what my mother kept repeating after I came out to her. "I should have known, I should have known...."

First, there is the traditional method of coming out, the "Good Dyke" method, which generally happens at the holidays. Lesbian Law #7 does state "When you come out, you must do so face to face preferably at Thanksgiving Dinner."

Why have our families become this necessary evil that we force ourselves to be around only at the holidays, so that those traditionally joyous times can be imprinted forever as horror stories of Uncle Ed puking on the turkey? Or perhaps Aunt Alice doing that table dance in front of the Christmas tree.

Or, maybe, that Easter you came home and stopped everyone's forks halfway to their mouths by saying, "Mom, Dad, everyone. I'm queer."

Just say no to ruining the holidays.

I have a particular fondness for the "Gentle" method. A bit less direct than other methods, but people will thank you once they get over the shock.

First, you can call your friends or family or whoever you are planning to come out to.

Yes! It's okay to tell someone over the phone.

Next, you bring up the subject of love, as in, "Guess what?! I've fallen in love!"

And they say, "With who?"

And you say, "Stephanie," or whatever your current lover's name is.

And your brother says, "Is that a unisex name?"

After the excitement dies down, the family will definitely thank you for your delicacy especially if you stress that you could have told everyone all at once at Thanksgiving and given Grandpa that heart attack.

Finally, there is the "Bold" method.

My brother has a friend named Duke. Duke is a hard workin', hard partyin', pop the top off the whiskey bottle and throw it out the pickup window on Friday after work type of guy.

One night, Duke and my brother were out drinking with a bunch of their redneck friends. About halfway through the evening, Duke was drunk and just itching for a fight. Someone told a gay joke and Duke jumped up.

"I'm gonna beat the crap out of you, man! I'm gonna beat the crap out of you!"

The guy just stared at him with his jaw in his lap and said in a small surprised voice, "Why?"

"'Cause I'm a fag, man!" Duke yelled and proceeded to fulfill his promise. Everyone enjoyed the fight and laughed it off as Duke having had too much to drink.

Later, Duke and my brother were sitting back sharing a bottle of Southern Comfort when my brother decided to get the real scoop. "So, Duke, what's the deal?"

And Duke replied, "I really am a fag, man."

Although this is a more direct, spur of the moment, get really drunk and spew all over the floor method, the lovely Lesbian Housewyfe does find this type of violence appealing. Perhaps if more people used this approach, there would be much less gay bashing and absolutely no fag jokes.

Know that one of my missions in life (along with a clean house and tasty meals) is to bring hope to the hidden lesbian housewyves of the world and maybe even affect others along the way.

When you need strength, just remember Lesbian Law #1: Never underestimate the power of a Lesbian Housewyfe.

No one in my family does.

And some of them don't even know.

Throw a Coming Out Cotillion

A cotillion is a tradition I've only really seen in the South, but anywhere there is "Society," there are cotillions. This ball was originally intended to display daughters and celebrate their "coming out into Society" when they reached a marriageable age. Yummy! I so wish to be put on display for all manner of men who can judge me and decide if I am "marriageable material."

But no matter the traditional sense! We are merely dealing with the ironic and clever use of the phrase "coming out into Society."

Ideally, I imagine our Coming Out Cotillion to be like this:

I'm standing at the top of a staircase in a beautiful ballgown, my sweet wyfe beside me in her gorgeous vintage tuxedo, surveying the glamorous ballroom below. An abundance of men and women fill the floor below, waltzing to a mixture of classical and popular music played by a live quartet wearing tuxedoes. Ballgowns merge with tuxedos as both men and women elegantly cross-dressed to the point that you can't tell who is who. We are all simply who we are.

And we are beautiful.

At a break in the music, we are announced by a man with a booming voice, "Mrs. And Mrs. Bourgeois-Reineke" and everyone turns to greet us as we elegantly stride down the stairs into the pack and join in the dancing.

Cucumber sandwiches and petit fours are served with champagne punch in the anterooms, with lemon water for those who have danced too much. The evening swirls on as more and more couples fill the ballroom, with the attending scandals and surprises. In the end, everyone leaves the ballroom and the magic dissolves as we all scramble back into our carriages and head home to sleep for the remaining couple of hours of darkness, now knowing who has been accepted into our society and who simply did not come (since all who came would be accepted).

Now, if a large banquet hall and string quartet are unavailable, I think you could simply use your own home. Insist that your guests wear formal clothing, and that cross-dressing is definitely permitted. Choose a fun mixture of classical and popular music emphasizing love and affection and Class-with-a-capital-c. Station someone at the door to announce people as they arrive, and make sure to use all your best china and crystal.

This is the time!

Pull out that punch bowl you never use!

If you want to get really southern, fill the thing with ginger ale and float lumps of lime sherbet in it for a real old-fashioned punch. Cut the crusts off of white bread and make cucumber sandwiches. Cube pound cake and coat in sugary icing to form petit fours. Pull back the carpet and move the furniture to the sides of the room for a big dancing floor. Provide plenty of water with thin slices of lemon to refresh your dancers. You might even get a dance instructor to teach everyone how to waltz.

The best part is celebrating the essence of what it means to "Come Out." The pitfalls and surprises and small moments of joy from meeting that true person inside your friend. The "Coming Out Cotillion" should be treated with respect and secrecy, and with joy and abandon.

Enjoy the party!

·❤·❤·❤·❤·❤·

A PERK OF THE LIFESTYLE

I am a housewyfe.

I am not a mother.

I know that, for many, these two concepts intertwine so synonymously that saying you are a housewyfe means that you are a full-time mother. I may look motherly, but I lost my figure to pie and cookies and homemade jam. I am most assuredly not a mother. I'm not even particularly maternal.

As the lovely Lesbian Housewyfe, I do respect every woman's right to choose to have a child. (Lesbian Law #27: "Breeding isn't just for breeders.") However, I also thank God every day that I can't "accidentally" have children. Lesbians work hard to have kids, and never ever will you hear a soon-to-be lesbian mother crying to her friends, wondering how this situation occurred.

She knows.

She was there.

A doctor was there along with a sperm-filled syringe.

Money changed hands.

Multiple visits occurred.

These women pursue the vocation of "mommy" with purpose.

That is not me. When I came out to my mother, she wailed, "I'll never have grandchildren!"

"What about my brother?"

She shot me a look that said, "Don't depend on him for nieces and nephews."

She knew that being a lesbian was my last out on motherhood. As a child, I didn't play with dolls. I asked for a little dolly that peed like a real baby one Christmas. The first soggy diaper doomed it. Straight to the bottom of the toy box with you!

And "Potty Dolly" never was seen again.

My brother did come through on the grandchildren front, so now my mother is "Nana" to a darling five-year-old boy.

Babies make me nervous. I dislike touching them. Plus, their fragility is legend with their weak little necks and inept little hands.

After all, I'm not called Grace for a very good reason. I would never be forgiven for dropping someone's baby. I mean, they would absolutely never speak to me again.

Also, babies unexpectedly explode.

Don't shake your head at me! You know it's true.

Babies alternately have poop, vomit, mucus, or drool spewing from their many orifices at any given time.

I visited an old friend with a new baby who, mid-lovely-visit to a quaint gourmet market, looked at her baby and said, "Oops! Poop explosion." She grimaced, picked the child up into her arms from the stroller and revealed the yellowy brown squishy stain rapidly rolling down the leg of its pants. She swiftly grabbed the diaper bag (babies cause extra baggage in so many ways!) and beelined it for the women's bathroom, where I can only imagine the carnage. She didn't return for twenty minutes.

Twenty minutes!

Twenty minutes of cleaning up poop from the child, the clothing, the fold-down diaper table, the women's restroom!

Ewww!

That could have happened on my lap.

Another of my maternal failures is that I cannot seem to sustain conversation with a baby. They will approach as they develop the means, and look up at me. I feel pressure to entertain.

"So," I say, "How's it going?"

The child looks at me and thrusts forward a little chubby hand containing something slimy: keys, a toy, a little catnip mouse they found on the floor.

"Unh!" They say. "Unh-unh!"

I accept the proffered object and they smile, or not. I hand it back and they drop it on my foot. The child toddles away. I kick the object somewhere else to dry before I pick it up again.

That's actually a pretty good encounter. Children sometimes cry, in which case I grasp them under their armpits and carry them at arms length to their Mom or Dad or designated overseer.

Maybe I'm not nervous. Maybe I'm just not comfortable. Babies move rapidly, make high-pitched noises and unexpectedly spew slime. Then they look at you with these little angelic smiles that break your heart.

You know what else does that? Demons in horror movies. Only they already have teeth.

My only defense? Treat them like adults. Get upset when they act like babies. "Don't be a child!" I'll say. "Act your age!"

Then I realize that their age is four or two or one. Embarrassed, I turn it into a joke. I tell them to be cool and ignore the entire conversation.

The Lesbian Housewyfe is just not a mom even though she seems maternal: baking cookies, crocheting baby afghans, puttering in the garden.

Remember Lesbian Law #1: Never Underestimate the Power of the Lesbian Housewyfe.

How do I have the time for all of these fun family activities?

No children.

·❤·❤·❤·❤·❤·

PARENTAL STRATEGIES

Nothing strikes fear into the hearts of homosexuals quite like a visit to the in-laws. Except perhaps a visit from the in-laws. Or maybe that time when your baby's Mom showed up on the front porch with all her stuff. Anyway, yours truly saw her parents make the trek all the way out to scenic Denver this past Christmas. Ah yes. My baby got hers (after that whole homeless Mom incident) as we gained the new year.

Actually, Mom, Dad, Steph, and I have worked out most of the really ooky nasty stuff so the visit was quite pleasant. We all just relaxed, sat back and had a good time. My family's favorite holiday customs include eating too much and watching too much television and we fulfilled our familial duty. Also, my mother and I shopped 'til we dropped. And then my father snatched me away to enjoy several good James Bond films.

Oh yes, Dad and I love ol' Puddinhead, as we call him. I know, I know. Lesbian Law #9: "Never promote anything which oppresses women." But, James is ridiculous! Plus, my Dad and I, we bond with Bond. It's yet another of the Lesbian Housewyfe's traditions.

Anyway, I have obviously developed a few strategies to deal with the old folks at home. I share them with you in penance for that whole James Bond addiction.

1. BE YOURSELF.

The biggest mistake most of us make when dealing with our parents is to fall back into those old patterns from our teenage years. I was the quiet good one in my family. I avoided problems. I smoothed over difficulties. I never washed a dish unless absolutely forced to. After our first visit with my Mom and Dad, my lovely wyfe looked at me and said, "Who the hell are you and what have you done with my lover?"

Then she began looking through my parent's guest room for the pod.

So remember, you are a different person now. As soon as I popped back into reality, I started speaking a new language, heavily influenced by that Lesbian Housewyfe phenonmenon, "Insta-truth." I know it's hard but parents can endure just about anything you can dish out. They are strong people. After all, they managed to live with you for several years-including the teenage ones. The Folks can take it.

My Mom and Dad took about a month to adjust, but the rest of our time together has worked out just fine. They respect me more now than they did when I first began this amazing trip with Stephanie and we can actually talk openly.

But not too openly. Boundaries have to be set somewhere.

After all, do you really want to hear about the sex life of people you have seen attempt to change into their pajamas without uncovering a single square inch of flesh? And they don't want to hear about your sex life since they spent a good portion of the beginning of their marriage changing your diapers. Puts a real kibosh on romance, let me tell you.

The most enjoyable element of this suggestion is rediscovering these people who raised you. Boundaries are created to be pushed against. Remember, they have more on you than you do on them.

They are holding all the nude baby pictures.

All you have to fight with is "Why did you do (fill in the blank) to me?"

Step away from that strategy and start collecting the dirt. They should pay for taking those photos.

2. LAUGH.

A major reason why we can't have good relationships with our parents is that we take them too seriously. I know I did. I discussed them. I analyzed their every move, word, and intonation. I analyzed my every move, word, and intonation. I discovered that I was becoming my mother. I screamed continuously for days on end with horror.

Then, my sweet Stephie, the love of my life, the shining angel in my existance, shook me until my head spun and said, "Get a grip!"

So I did.

Thank goodness.

I suddenly discovered, as I stepped away from the whole situation and began accepting that I was who I was-even the parts that are like my mother, that my parents are funny people. They have their own special quirks which really can be considered humorous. If you saw them on a sit-com, I know you would laugh.

For example, when I came out to my Mom, she was totally against the whole idea. She kept saying, "But LA, I just don't think you truly are a lesbian."

Finally, exasperated and running out of arguments (I was down to, "Well, Ma. I'm having lots of sex with a woman and really enjoying it. What do you think that means?"), I said, "Ma, I think you're floating down that big river in Egypt."

She replied, "What?"

"Denial."

She let out this giant bark of laughter, stopped herself, and said, "That's not funny."

I think we can all agree that this whole exchange provides and example of exactly the type of humorous people your parents could be if given half a chance. The Folks can be funny. Even if they don't mean to.

Start slowly. Get a good look at your parents. There has to be one funny thing about them. Maybe it's their ears. Ears are always a good place to start. They have to be the funniest looking thing on everyone's body. Of course, good ears turn me on, but then again, I like to laugh. Soon you will find yourself chuckling about the fact that Dad drinks too much, and making fun of him by doing imitations of him stumbling home drunk late at night. Perhaps you'll even do your performance in front of him.

It could happen.

Anyway, if all else fails, maybe your Mom has a big nose. I lost out on that count. Lucky she has that wicked sense of humor.

3. HAVE SEX WHILE YOUR PARENTS ARE IN THE NEXT ROOM SLEEPING.

Now, I know this is hard. Bite the bullet.

But, do be sure they are asleep.

Remember, June knows best. After all, isn't Lesbian Law #1: "Never Underestimate the Power of the Lesbian Housewyfe."?

My family loves me. And so does Steph's.

Grandma's Biscuits

I have lived off of this recipe for most of my life, so much so that even my wedding vows included "I promise to bake biscuits for you."

At this point, I suppose they bear little resemblance to the lovely pillows of goodness that my grandmother used to pull out of the oven each morning. My transgressions include the substitution of butter for shortening, along with an addition of sugar.

So far, Grandmother hasn't been so horrified as to emerge from heaven to come down and discipline me for the sacrilege. Of course, she was a very forgiving woman and quite used to making due.

1 1/2 cups all-purpose flour
1/2 teaspoon salt
1/2 teaspoon baking soda
1 1/2 teaspoons baking powder
1 tablespoon sugar
3 tablespoons butter
1/2 cup whole milk or buttermilk

Sift together dry ingredients. Cut in the butter with a pastry cutter or two knives or a big fork or whatever is convenient. I've even seen ladies smush up the butter and flour with their fingers, but this recipe benefits from handling the dough very little, so I never attempted it. Anyway, get the bits of butter down in size so that they are no bigger than small peas. Mix in the milk quickly. The dough should be moist.

Turn out the dough onto a floured board and knead just enough to hold the dough together. Roll out to 1/4" thick and cut with a 1 1/2" biscuit cutter. Place on a greased cookie sheet and bake in a preheated

450 degree oven for 10 – 12 minutes.

Feeling extra decadent? Pour a little oil on the cookie sheet before placing the biscuits and coat both sides of each biscuit with the oil before sliding them to their places. Then bake.

Yummy.

·♥·♥·♥·♥·♥·

MITZVOT

A couple of years ago, Stephanie and I got invited to a "Seder and Kugel Cookoff" for Passover. Like good little gentiles (Lesbian Law #6: "Celebrate diversity in all its forms."), we did extensive research on the internet and our cookbook archive for recipes. We settled on two, one matzoh and one potato.

Chicken fat sizzled in the large cast iron skillet while Steph peeled and grated the potatoes and onions. (My favorite helpful hint from a reader on Epicurious was to use bacon drippings in lieu of chicken fat. Soooo not kosher.)

I soaked matzoh to blend it into the apples, raisins and apricots for my sweet casserole dripping with butter, sugar and cinnamon. We slipped both of them into the oven and crossed our fingers. They both came out golden, crisp and brown.

I liberated a red Spanish table wine from my wine rack and I brought that along for dinner. I totally gained points with our hostess, Sureva, by allowing that this choice was inspired by the Sephardim (Jews from Spain or Portugal, especially those exiled from those countries in the late 15th century—Thanks to The Ghost of Hannah Mendes by Naomi Ragen).

"I didn't know you had Jewish heritage."

"I don't. I just finished a novel." Sheepish smile and thrusting forth of wine bottle.

She took the wine, extracted the author and title from me (see above), and disappeared to greet other guests.

Whew. Passed my test!

A large table in the center of the living room quickly filled with sweet and savory kugels, noodle, matzoh and potato, brought by a bunch of whitebread gentiles just like me: pink-skinned and feeling a little bit guilty about missing the next day's Easter services because of a Passover Hangover.

The kugels beckoned as we learned the rules of the contest. Two votes each, and cast your votes by sticking a toothpick into your favorite after tasting all of them (Tasting, mind you! We have a full dinner ahead!).

We circulated and scooped small bites of each kugel onto our tiny paper plates. By the end, a couple of kugels looked like porcupines while others stood lonely, not even one vote from the person who made them! Luckily, ours did not suffer that fate. I voted for myself, and Steph's potato kugel was given perhaps the greatest compliment imaginable by Sureva: "Your kugel tastes just like my mother's." The potato kugel received several toothpicks.

We stepped back from the table and sipped some tasty kosher wine. (Yes, I did say "tasty kosher wine." Some good kosher wines are being bottled these days, and they are now available year-round at our favorite local wine shop.) The surprise of the evening was Nate, then only eighteen, being crowned the King of Kugel. "Unfair," some of us cried; our voices muffled by mouths full of his tasty offering.

Next, we ambled over to a large L-shaped arrangement of tables and enjoyed a traditional Seder dinner accompanied by all the kugels. Our hostess made copies of the service for us to read aloud in turns, progressing around the table one paragraph at a time.

"Why is this night different from every other night?"

For starters, I found out what a kugel was. And made one!

We departed carrying one half-empty container of apple-matzoh kugel which went into the refrigerator for a month (We were kugeled out!) before finally being sent to the great round black kugel heaven (otherwise known as the garbage can) on my front patio.

I must admit, I deposited it there without much thought. The bushes were just beginning to leaf out in early May and I had triumphantly finished my spring cleaning that afternoon.

In the middle of the night, Tux, our border collie, barked at the patio door. Sleep befuddled me and I lay there blinking myself awake while Steph stumbled to the door.

"Tux. I'm up. Thank you. Good dog." Steph pulled back the curtain covering the glass door and her tone changed. "Oh my God."

At this point, my sweet honey-bunny has noted that I should tell you we live in the middle of town. Downtown. Securely in the midst of town. Our sweet little house is arranged with other sweet little houses, all with house numbers, on a paved street with a name in our little mountain town.

Because we live in town (in case I haven't made that clear enough), the last thing I expected Stephanie to say was:

"Bear."

I sat straight up and made myself a little "bed-wobbly" as I realized that the continuing sounds of crashing and bumping were actually a bear going through our trash. "Bear?" I regained my balance and ran over to the door to peer uneasily out the curtain.

The bear was halfway into the trashcan about eight feet away from us. She tossed out bits of trash, dragged out a particularly interesting morsel, sat back on her haunches, and snarfed it down, daintily leaving the plastic wrap or bag or container on the ground.

Steph and I looked at each other. As fascinating as this was, a bear sat on our front stoop strewing garbage everywhere. We had to do something.

"Let's turn the light on. That should scare it away."

Two floodlight bulbs cover the patio area with light. We never turn them on because we like to sleep in the dark, but desperate times call for desperate measures, as the ubiquitous "they" say.

A flip of the switch and light illuminated a black bear, probably about four to five feet at the shoulder (not standing on her hind legs) when she untucked herself from the garbage can.

That's big. I mean, really big. A big black bear.

She pulled another tasty bit from the trashcan and blinked as the light hit her face. She turned her big bear head toward us and dipped her chin a little as if to say, "Thanks. It was a little dark out here." Then, she went back to chomping on.... Kugel! She was eating the remnants of the matzoh kugel!

Steph looked at me.

I looked at her.

"Bear Mitzvah!"

The bear peered briefly at the two crazy naked ladies giggling in the plate glass door and returned to her rumination.

In the morning, after picking the garbage out of our yard, we drove to the hardware store and bought a large rolling bear-proof trash. Outfitted with a metal strap around the lid and cables with trigger snap hooks which attach to the metal tabs poking through metal lined slots on the top, this trashcan completely thwarts the bear (at least our black bear). Bears come back to where they've found food before, so for a while we found this trashcan turned over on its side in the yard or standing on its head on the patio.

However, since we installed this tough trashcan, we've never found any actual garbage in our lawn.

And finally, after a full summer, she's given up on us.

I may only be a housewyfe, but I can outsmart a bear.

And cater her "bear mitzvah."

KEEPING BEARS OUT OF YOUR TRASH

After our encounter with the bear, we purchased the bear-proof trashcan and that took care of the majority of the issue. However, I did some research to discover what else I could do to keep the bears out.

In the springtime, bears are coming out of hibernation and just can't resist any sort of food. If you must leave your trashcan outside like me, you should definitely invest in a bear-proof trashcan to avoid my experience. While the actual encounter was quite exciting, repeats of the experience can lead not only to a yard full of trash, but a bolder bear happily trotting back day after day to see what new items you've put into the buffet.

Yikes!

Last summer, someone in my town came home to find a bear happily scarfing down peanut butter in her pantry. I can't imagine anyone who wouldn't find this quite a shock.

So, now you have your bear-proof trashcan and a frustrated bear. To keep the odors down in the trashcan, either make sure to only clean out the fridge on trash day or get some lime. Not limes like in margaritas, but lime like calcium oxide.

You'll remember in William Faulkner's short story, "A Rose for Emily," when the townspeople think Miss Emily has a dead animal under her house, they sneak in and pour lime all over the basement. Later, of course, we all find out that she was keeping that dead body upstairs. Ewww!

However, the reason for this is that lime absorbs or covers the odors of decomposing organics like dead bodies or old bits of steak. Equal opportunity odor reducer!

Make sure to use organic garden lime to reduce any potential dangers. Once the odors disappear, the bear should too. She's not interested in anything but food, and the reduction of that availability will keep her away more than anything else.

Okay, now the bear is out of your garbage, but still visiting your neighbors. Quickly solve this problem with midnight lime dropping in their trashcan, or just share these handy tips with them.

Good luck!

·♥·♥·♥·♥·♥·

Springtime Makeover

I am sitting in the sun in a ragged piece of lawn furniture. The brick red paint is chipping off the soft wood and the pillow which kindly softens the slatted backrest and woven seat has lost gobs of its stuffing. I don't care. The rays from the sun are warming the top of my head and a slight breeze is tickling my nose with some of my own hair.

Around me the grass is deepening to green again. Almost all the brown which was so prevalent only last month has been excommunicated. Pink tulips with white edging burst from a corner of the backyard. Daffodils permeate my sidewalk boxes. Dandelions sprinkle the lawn.

Cleo, our small Siamese, rolls over and over in the dirt and leftover fall leaves, crushing the tender greens from an unknown bulb. She rises, her eyes still crossed in ecstasy, and settles in a sunbeam.

I close my eyes and take a deep breath. Smells reach my nose; freshly turned dirt, sweet grass cuttings, and a hint of rain.

Spring is here.

I look across the lawn and spot Mookie, the poodle we babysit. She's still all fuzzed out from the winter. Her curly brown hair fluffs out in an all over poodle afro. She sits in her own patch of sun, mouth slightly open to release the heat.

It's time for Mookie's spring makeover.

The first step in this process is convincing Mookie's mom that it's not too early to cut the dog's hair. She hates change in any shape or form, so this is not an easy task. We only win by noting the escalating temperature repeatedly and citing doggy health tips which pertain to grooming. Finally, she gives in with great reluctance after we threaten to take Mookie to the groomer during the day when she has no control. As Mookie's mom has a mysterious but adamant fear of professional groomers, this tactic usually works.

Second is scheduling. This process is decided through long discussions which go much like this:

Us: "So, when is good for you?"

Mookie's Mom: "Well, we need a whole afternoon."

Us: "So, when is good for you?"

Mookie's Mom: "Well, it should be a sunny and warm day."

Us: "So, when is good for you?"

Mookie's Mom: "Well, when is good for you?."

It's worse than trying to get a group of lesbians to decide on a restaurant. (Lesbian Law #12: "Every decision must involve everyone who will be affected by that decision. The best way to structure the discussion is to sit down as a group and get everyone's opinion. This decision making process should be used in every situation, no matter how small or seemingly insignificant the subject matter.")

Finally, a date is set with complete understanding for things like sudden romances and sunny day disease as long as a phone call is in the offing. One slip up on Mookie's mom's part and the groomer (one Stephanie, also known as my sweet honey bunny) must be bribed with sushi dinners and breakfasts at the Mercury Cafe, a bohemian bistro with great atmosphere and even better food.

Finally, the gathering occurs. A large bath towel is taped to our dining room table. Mookie's mom brings over the dog and assorted

implements of grooming. Scissors are tested for sharpness. Combs &
brushes are laid out, cleaned and at the ready. The clippers are plugged
in and oiled. A lint brush is laid to the side for final cleanup of the
towel.

It is time.

Get the poodle.

Two large, intelligent, powerful women set out in search of the dog
who knows what is about to happen.

Unfortunately for the poodle, the humans know her hiding places.
They quickly find her and carry her small struggling body to the table.
It takes both of them to get her settled.

Now we begin. Mookie has three different emotional stages during
the grooming ritual.

1. DENIAL (1 HOUR)

Mookie's denial stage is pretty calm. She tries to look cute and just
ignore the fact that her mom is collaborating with her second most
favorite person in the world to shave her entire body. Eventually, she
begins to feel cooler and must acknowledge that the strange whirring
noise is connected to the clumps of fur which are dropping onto the
table.

The stage is ending when Mookie begins to try to appease the
humans. She licks their hands while they are clipping her. A naive
person might say, "Oh how sweet. She loves us." We know this means,
"Oh, please stop! What did I ever do to deserve this?" This pathetic
little lick is accompanied with little poodle trembles as the chill of the
air sets in against her newly clipped hairs.

The humans have been at it for awhile. They're tired. I get them
iced tea while they let the poodle run. She looks like a miniature

deranged lion charging through the house to her favorite hiding place. All the other pets block her path by gathering and commenting on her horrible haircut.

The humans return and quickly make the capture.

2. ANGER (UNTIL SHE GETS DISCIPLINED)

Having been released once, the poodle is reluctant to begin again. She immediately begins the licking tactic. As this is basically useless, the struggling begins. Yipping barks which don't quite exceed the hearing of humans pierce the air. The valiant amateur groomers struggle with a poodle which weighs approximately one zillionth of their combined body weight. When they finally immobilize her and start clipping once again, she snaps at them, yipping and flinching when the clippers come too near her fur. The snapping causes a curious change in Mookie's mom who grabs Mookie by the scruff of the neck and gives her a short tug.

Mookie realizes she is trapped.

3. ACCEPTANCE (20 MINUTES)

The final moments of the clip are spent in weakened acceptance of her fate. The human clip her face, trimming her mustache and finding just the right slope for her ears.

She is finally done. Mookie is about one third her original size. Her sleek body is revealed and the few decorative touches acknowledged. The puffball on top of her head and her rounded ears frame her face well and you remember why they called them "poodle-do's" in high school. She retains her schnauzer mustache and a small poof of fur at the end of her tail. She resembles a small deer as she gracefully bounds off the table to remove herself from the close vicinity of the humans. Her newfound agility is tested as her pawpads reach the floor and she no longer skids across the linoleum on her trek to the pet door.

The humans smile at each other in recognition of a job well done.

I refill their iced tea glasses and smile gently. After all, Lesbian Law #1 is "Never underestimate the power of a Lesbian Housewyfe."

A gentle spring snow begins to fall outside the window.

SWEET ICED TEA

Each spring, I pull out my gallon pitcher and start making this elixir again. This classic southern drink reminds me of lying on the couch in my Grandmother's house while she watched *The Price Is Right*. My sweet honey-bunny and I keep it around at all times, at her behest. This is when you know you've married the right woman.

1 quart boiling water
3 quarts warm water
1/4 cup sugar
2 family sized teabags

Put sugar in the bottom of a gallon iced tea container. Pour in warm water. Add tea bags. Then pour the boiling water over the tea bags. Leave out until the tea is the color you prefer. Put into the refrigerator and wait until cold or pour over ice in a tall glass for immediate refreshment.

I like to add a dollop of lemon juice to get that good Grandma taste.

·♥·♥·♥·♥·♥·

CHANGE OF ADDRESS

M oving is traumatic.

I wish I could soften this blow somehow, but even the Lesbian Housewyfe has to admit that uprooting your entire household and taking it somewhere else, even if it is just next door, is not as easy as we all wish. Whether you have a truckload full of professional movers or a handful of drunk friends, the experience is always memorable. That's just the nature of moving.

As theological offspring (secular translation: a preacher's kid), I began moving at an early age. My valuable moving lessons included Possessions Can Be Transient (if one is or isn't careful with the breakables), Your Childhood Room Defined Through Your Presence, and How to Pack and Move An Entire House in One Month. Recently I was able to put my extensive knowledge of moving to good use as Stephie and I made our first move as an old married couple.

The beginning of our moving process plays like a soap opera. This particular morality play brings to light the plight of the renter in the 90's.

Renter, of course, meaning, "Landless rabble who give a portion of their income (after taxes) currently at the rate of 25% to the landholder of their choice. Alternate definition: Those who throw money down a rathole."

In our case, the house we were living in was sold out from underneath us. The new landlord (Skippy, a.k.a. The Evil One) increased our rent geometrically and took away all our storage space. We got out of there as quickly as we could, which is to say about four months. The process went something like this. I can't be entirely specific because the most wretched memories are quickly being repressed, even as I write this.

I began by setting aside the last month for packing and finding a new house. I would have begun packing earlier but, for some strange reason, both Stephie and her mother had a definitively negative reaction to the suggestion of living out of our suitcases for three months. Also, searching for a new house to lease doesn't really work out more than a month before move-in because of the quick turnover of properties. No one wants to leave their rental property vacant for two or three months until your lease is up.

Funny that.

Anyway, as my self-imposed deadline slid up with the silence of a snake in the grass, I gathered boxes. All kinds of boxes. Big, small, found, bought, cardboard, and plastic. My favorite were the big plastic 18 gallon storage boxes which one can easily find on sale at Target or K-Mart (or WalMart I suppose. We didn't really have one handy here, but I used to frequent them all the time when I lived back in Arkansas.)

Some of the most handy, though, were the 32 gallon plastic trash cans with the little wheels on the bottom. I moved my whole kitchen with those and didn't nick one dish or break one glass. And my movers were the handful of drunk kind. One of the unfortunate side effects of this behavior is that I still scour the Sunday advertisements for sales on those big plastic storage boxes. I just can't help it.

I also snuck around and packed things while no one was watching. Stephanie and her mother started getting that "deer caught in headlights" look whenever they heard me say, "When was the last time you used this?" Everything over a year out of use was either stuck into a pile to sell or packed away into one of our big plastic boxes. I was pretty ruthless. Or so I thought until I got into our new house and found about ten thousand things I should have just thrown away. Of course, who knows when you will next need a cute little egg cup made with a chicken foot as a base? These are the types of things which can unexpectedly come in handy, you think as you pack it.

What was I thinking?

As our allotted time in the old house dwindled, we began looking for a new place. I can't tell you how many houses I walked through. We sorted through the newspaper ads using our highly selective criteria (two bedrooms and cheap!), made phone calls, and set appointments.

I looked at full houses, duplexes, apartments and ratholes where you wouldn't send a dog to sleep. I questioned owners about gardening (Can we dig up the yard?), pets (Our two cats are really well behaved and completely litter trained. Really.), and what services they paid. I talked to people from one end of the spectrum to the other.

When I thought I couldn't go on, a wonderful little dyke came along with a cute little house and said all the right little things. Don't you just love it when you meet someone who does that? She even gave us an invaluable week of overlap. Of course, she knows Lesbian Law #16: "Rent your house to 'Family' whenever possible."

Lord knows, we need to stick together.

When the search had finally ended, we gathered the forces which consisted of a handful of students (who came to help in return for free beer), friends (who came to help in return for free beer), and indentured servants (who came to help because we helped them).

Stephanie's mom found a guy who would rent his enormous moving truck out for almost pennies and we set the date, the Saturday before Memorial Day.

As with all good moving days, it rained. We persevered however and, with the help of Dunkin' Donuts, Pizza Hut, and the Miller Brewing Company, got every one of our large things moved on that very day. The small moving party went well and everyone cleared out in time for us to go back and retrieve the cats from the old house. When we walked in, they were staring at the door. I can tell you, the ride back to our new house was quite noisy. Once we got there though, they were pretty happy. The new house has carpeted floors, a nap-time luxury at our old house. Everyone settled in quickly.

The last week before the move-out deadline at our old house, we gathered odds and ends which would fit into a small Plymouth Horizon and transported them back to be unpacked. Plants, small but awkwardly packing objects, and the most fragile knick-knacks were moved this way. The rest of the stored things were smushed into a rented moving van and trucked across town. On the night before the last day, we cleaned that old sweet house from top to bottom.

I felt a strange sadness in the pit of my stomach as I closed the door. I had never put so much work into a house. This place had been our first home. I learned to garden here. The vivid memories of my first household came flooding into my mind as I took one last look. The first tomatoes devoured greedily off the vine. Losing all my basil last year because I didn't make the pesto quickly enough. Finding that I really did enjoy the quiet zenlike quality of the cleaning process. Having my wonderful Stephanie give me the space to write again.

Fortunately, the feeling was fleeting because I really was too busy to dwell.

Stephanie did the walk-through with the old landlord the next day and at approximately noon, mountain standard time, we were free. Free as the breeze. Free from Skippy (a.k.a. The Evil One), free from the burden of such a big house (our new one is nice and cozy), and free from my mother-in-law!

Oh yes, during this time, she moved out to a whole new house by herself! I mean, I love her but, well, have you ever tried living with your mother-in-law? I can't recommend it. Especially in those first few months when you're still shifting the balance of the chores and wondering what brand of milk your honey likes the best.

But now we are in our new house, unpacking. Y'know, it took a month for us to pack and now I find we've taken a month to unpack. We're almost done now! And my theory seems to have held up because, when one undertakes a new task, it always pays to remember Lesbian Law #1: "Never Underestimate the Power of a Lesbian Housewyfe."

Now, where should I put my garden?

Hints for Making the Move

As a young child of ministers, I've moved many, many times. The science of moving from one abode to another contains many twists and turns, and can show off your organizational skills, or lack thereof.

A wise friend of mine went out and bought two large wheeled trashcans right before she moved. She packed the two cans full of her dishes, pots, pans and other assorted items from her kitchen. Then she simply wheeled the heavy cans into the moving van, and moved. Upon reaching her new abode, she unpacked her kitchen and then started using the trashcans as trashcans.

Multipurposing at its best!

I followed her example during my early moves and added my own twist. I began to scour the paper for sales on those large plastic storage boxes and purchasing them as I could. They stacked neatly inside each other for storage when we weren't moving and then filled quickly and neatly for safe transport of many fragile items. With our final move to an actual house that we own, we began to actually use these boxes for storage.

The best ideas for moving are really the simplest:

Use commonsense when packing.

Don't pack your suitcases one inside of the other. Pack them with your clothes.

Pack books and other small heavy objects in small boxes so you aren't breaking your back picking up a giant heavy box.

Rent or borrow a dolly to transport boxes and large pieces of furniture from the house to the moving van and back.

And, if at all possible, pay people to move your stuff for you.

·♥·♥·♥·♥·♥·

PRO-GRASS-TINATION BLUES

Every year, we have a moment where the snow melts, and the earth begins to smell again. Not in a bad way, simply that dirt smell we lose when the ground freezes. Just past Easter, the ski mountain closes and green grass miraculously takes the place of the snow. Crocuses show their dainty heads, then grape hyacinth in bunches of dazzling purple. Daffodils and then tulips pop up in shades of pink, red and yellow.

I am sitting on my front porch in a turquoise wicker rocker. The chair wraps around me and I lean into the firm cushion as a light breeze ruffles my womanly leg hair. On this warm and sunny day, the zephyr reveals my mountain location with its chilly touch. Aspens' leaves rustle in the gentle wind. Poppies bud under the pink canopy of the crabapple tree, and the lilacs begin their charge out of the gates. With their full unveiling next weekend, the air will take on the scent of Fruit Stripe gum (the grape flavor) when the lilacs' odor melds with the smell of fresh run-off melting snow flowing down the many streams throughout Steamboat Springs.

Asiago, my golden kitty boy, leaps into the air, spinning like a circus performer in his attempt to catch a bee. He lands among the white puffy dandelion seedheads, up to his belly in grass, and I realize the awful truth.

I have to do something about my lawn.

In the past, I have been a dandy gardening housewyfe. I had a beautiful crop of veggies in Denver, and count farmers in my heritage, strong southern folk who grew their own food out of necessity. My mother spent many years creating vegetable beds out of lawns at each parsonage we inhabited.

I can remember standing in one particularly scary patch she was attempting to reclaim, staring at a weed as big as me. It glowered down threateningly at my little five year old self. Mom yelled over without raising her head, "Go on! Pull it! It won't bite."

I stared at the weed and grasped it at the very tip-top of the stem, pulling with all of my might. I leaned back, and it leaned with me. The weed slipped through my grasp, sending me tumbling backwards onto my butt in the muddy soil. Its triumph was short-lived as my mother reached over and deftly pulled the thing from the dense Arkansas soil.

My hero!

"You have to pull from the bottom."

To her credit, she didn't laugh in my presence. And I did eventually, kicking and screaming, learn how to weed.

I still hate it. I think every gardener does.

I know, I know. Lesbian Law #26: "I will grow all of my own vegetables throughout every season possible, using only organic methods, in appreciation and emulation of Mother Earth."

That means weeding.

Sigh.

There is one week in the springtime when my yard goes from beautiful to out-of-control. Unfortunately, this week always coincides with my desire to spend more time outside on my porch, watching the neighbors drive by and the pets frolic through my yard. My beautiful view of the front yard means that I can no longer deny it.

I have to do something about my lawn.

Many gardeners tell me that "the best defense is a good offense" meaning that I should start weeding when the weeds are tiny so I won't have to work as hard. However, none of them have managed to teach me the difference between the weed seedlings and the actual plant seedlings. I mean really. They all look the same to me.

Is that racist? Or plantist? Or just specious?

I'm a liar. I can identify the dandelions. They stare at me, happily defiant, staking out their new territory with their little paratroopers. I sigh as I watch their seeds soar through the air, spreading the scourge to my neighbor's lawn. There was a time, about ten years ago, when I made a pact with myself that I would not allow my dandelions to spread to other yards.

Lesbian Law #25: "Never impose on others unless your civil rights are in danger."

With the advent of the full-time job and, well, life I suppose, I have broken this pact many times over. Right now, my dandelions are puffing their way to world domination. I have so many; I've been investigating dandelion wine. At least I could get drunk, and then I wouldn't care if the lawn needs weeding.

But I object to attending 12-step programs, so I guess that's out.

Sigh.

I have to do something about my lawn.

The columbines are weaving their way through tall grass in the little garden lining my porch, sending out blooms amid stalks of tall grass. Bunches of strawberry leaves fluffily sned their alien feelers to invade my columbine bed. The entire porch garden is a war zone as I see dandelions sprout from the midst of the strawberry patch. Soon, I will be forced to arm myself with a hand spade, a small soil fork, and a dandelion digger, pull on my purple suede gardening gloves and head out to do battle.

The dandelions launch their offensive by digging in so deeply I can't reach the base of their roots with my digger. I pull dandelions raggedly, leaving an inch or two of root behind, knowing that I'll be forced to return in the coming months. The grass I grasp in mighty handfuls, digging and scratching with my fork until the soil releases its hold on the roots. They come up in clumps, and I now need to replace all the soil that I just threw away with the roots. The dandelions, thistles, and some of the grass go into the garbage.

Yep, you heard me right: the trash can. Don't dump your weeds in the compost pile if they have already formed their seedheads. Then they just proliferate throughout your garden everywhere you fertilize with your black gold. Compost is not something to be tainted with weeds. I get enough from the wind, rodents and birds to last me a lifetime. I don't need any appearing due to my own insertion.

Sigh.

I've got to do something about my lawn.

I've created a list, as I do every year.

This year, I'm going to mow the lawn. Correction, this year, I'm going to get the neighbor kid to mow the lawn for $10 a week.

My half-barrel planter needs to be righted and filled with beautiful flowers.

The swing built by my grandfather needs to be moved into the front yard, and the porch transformed from a repository for snow shovels to the summer haven we adore. We spend four to six hours a day on this porch on our summertime weekends, and we need that retreat...soon.

The mint bucket needs to be weeded and renewed with more varieties. As every good gardener knows, you must isolate your mint plants or they will take over the yard, invasive and fresh smelling little stinkers! Mine are in a wash tub that I've filled with dirt and dubbed "the mint bucket." I'm fully prepared for mojitos. Except for the weeding.

Having the front haven means the eviction of the weeds from the little garden lining the porch. Meant to highlight the columbine (state plant of Colorado!), our little patch is currently filled with any columbine who can overcome the giant stalks of grass and the encroachment of the nearby strawberry patch where the neighborhood dogs enjoy napping. Each year we attempt to thwart the dogs by installing cheap edging – which generally works - but last year the edging didn't get pulled out, and ended up wrapped around the blades of the snowblower.

Oops.

I need to weed the front porch garden, the driveway garden, the edge of the sidewalk, and the small rock garden by the street. Then, I can start on the back yard. Speaking of which....

Clouds from the south are moving north, carrying the promise of an extra day of avoidance. Today, though, I need to make sure that the neighbor boy won't break his ankle in the grass-disguised hole in our backyard (he'd never come back!), so I make myself start the gardening season with a quick shovel of dirt.

First, I have to find my gloves. This trek, by itself, could take all afternoon. I attempt to remember where I left them and manage to discover their hiding place in the loft.

Whooping with triumph, I bop my way down the steep stairway and perfectly fit them onto my chubby little fingers. The old caked mud makes it hard for me to close my hand, but shaping a few fists works out the kinks. Now for the shovel.

I exit the house back onto the front porch for the shovel, and flip-flop my way around the house to rediscover the location of the "danger hole." Since I'm actually searching for the hole, I manage to find it by catching a toe.

Limping around the side of the house in my unfortunate footwear, the old nasty compost left by the previous owner catches my eye. Perfect to fill the hole! Right now, the leaves of our lilac hedge shroud this particular pile, and a respectable number of weeds have sprouted out of its top despite the dense shadow. I begin my archaology and discover the lilac protects its own as the low hanging branches diminish each shovel full of dirt.

Flip-flop, flip-flop across the back lawn. Dump the meager load of dirt into the ever-deepening hole. Flip-flop back to do battle with the lilac for my soil. Fifteen minutes later, I'm done. Dirt gets brushed off the shovel and the now clean tool stores away in the tall plastic storage shed on my back deck. Gloves off to re-enter civilization.

Whew. Almost didn't make it back.

Kettle of water to the stove, fill my small teapot with leaves and soon I settle back with my warm cup of tea on the front porch. This is my favorite part of gardening.

I think unusually favorably upon my ex-brother-in-law who, searching for a compliment for my lawn, said, "I like it. It's....organic."

He knows Lesbian Law #1: "Never underestimate the power of a lesbian housewyfe."

I've got to do something about my lawn.

Mojito Rewards

1 T fresh mint leaves, whole

1 oz. Light rum

1 oz. Freshly squeezed Lime juice

1 oz. Simple syrup (equal parts water and sugar, heated to dissolve sugar and then cooled), or you can go traditional and use a tablespoon of superfine sugar.

Ice

Club Soda

There are tons of ways that people prepare this drink. Traditionally, you muddle (or smash) the mint and the sugar together with the lime juice. Add rum and ice and then fill the tall glass to the brim with your club soda. I make it a little easier by using simple syrup and simply bruising the leaves in the juice and syrup at the bottom of the glass with a long ice tea spoon for the first step.

At the end, everyone does the same thing – sip and relax on a hot afternoon.

· ❤ · ❤ · ❤ · ❤ · ❤ ·

THE GARDEN

Sunlight penetrates my eyelids, turning the darkness underneath soft pink. I turn away from its unforgiving gaze and snuggle in a little deeper. My partner sighs and allows me to wrap myself around her, pulling her beautiful body close. We fit together, every bend and crevice melding together as a godsent gift.

After a moment, the July sun makes me too hot to snuggle or sleep anymore and I turn to look at the clock. 8:30. A huge sleep-rumpled flame-point cat crawls from underneath my bed. He stretches his long majestic body and opens his gaping maws of death in a terrifying yawn. I follow suit. His girlfriend, Cleo, leans out from her perch on my pillow, tilting her tiny Siamese head to check out Rhett's movements and giving a soft meow of protest to me at the same time. I kiss my partner's soft shoulder, secure her tea request, and rise to make our morning cups of hot tea, Earl Grey for me and Irish Breakfast for her.

Ah yes, the midsummer gardening slump. We are finally at the point where my planting is done, the weeding is never done, and watering is a way of life. Waiting is the name of the game. For some reason, I can't get my garden to start producing a little at a time all during the summer. My way seems to be to have the entire garden come in all at once at the end of the summer, overflowing my cupboards, and sending me on frantic searches for canning supplies.

But for now, I can take some time to relax.

Gardening season starts in early January, when the seed catalogs come in. I pour through the pages like a wino slurping a gallon bottle. Johnny's, Seeds of Change, and Burpee feed my soul with their bright colors, gardening instructions, and the promise of spring seedlings. I find myself attracted to strange new plants that would never fit into my color scheme and eventually are crossed off the list as too expensive and unneeded. Lots of ornamentals go this way.

I think I have a thing with flowers. Vegetables, fruits and herbs seem necessary since you eat them, but flowers seem so...frilly. Every year I go through my seed catalogs with my little pencil and circle the seeds I want, going wild in the flower section. Every year I say to myself, only a couple of flowers, we can't spend that much money. Every year I am very disciplined about how many seeds I will allow myself.

So every year, I end up buying at least one flat of flowers to fill up an empty space in my yard.

I am a young gardener. I haven't recognized my addictions yet.

The excitement mounts when the actual seeds arrive. I rip open each envelope (or box!) and run my fingers over the packets. Stephie is called into action as I shove each packet into her face saying, "Ooh! Ooh! Look! Here's that tomato I told you about. And what about this pepper? Isn't it going to be fantastic? Oh jeez. I forgot I ordered this. It's a surprise for you, sweetheart. Johnny-Jump-Ups."

At this point, she is required by law (Lesbian Law # 11: Value and treasure every remark your partner utters (serious or silly) and back her up, if need be.) to say, "Oh sweetie. Thanks." before she escapes back to her work.

I hop around the house for a couple of weeks reading instructions, gathering supplies, and scheduling. As I start the actual planting, I get to feeling a bit guilty because of the sweet little seeds I'm having to leave out of the earth for a time, but I know it will pass. I would feel worse if I planted them to early and they never came up.

Tomatoes get to be planted right away, so maybe this year they will come out earlier. All the herbs, too! They can be transplanted into pots easily and are usually the first to be removed from the growlights and put under natural sunlight. Peppers need to wait until March, depending on your last frost date. It gets really confusing sometimes.

But always wait and plant your pumpkins, squash, zucchini, and peas directly into the earth. I learned this the hard way. I killed my zucchini and my transplanted squash was the size of a small orange.

You have to work at that in Colorado.

Now, as my little seedlings expand, I prepare my dirt. Nothing can really compare to working directly in the earth.

When I was a small child, I used to play in the dirt, like we all did. One day, however, I was playing with my little brother in a big mud puddle and somehow we got this idea. Mom always encouraged us to finger-paint, so what was the difference between using finger-paint on paper and mud on the side of the house. Unfortunately, we chose the side that faced the church and a section near a window where Mom was doing whatever Mom did.

I was five.

I had no idea.

Needless to say, I learned my lesson and now I use a spade fork to turn dirt, a shovel to move it, and compost to fertilize it. Never, never, never do I use my dirt to paint handprint turkeys (since they are so easy to make) on the side of the house.

Especially since I am the one who has to clean it up now.

However, I do, sometimes, run through the sprinkler on hot days.

We can't be grown up all the time.

Now that the soil is prepared and the seedlings are bursting from their pots, it's time to put them in the ground outside!!!! After a hardening off period where I slowly expose my babies to the harsh outdoors, I carefully put each seedling in its own special place which I have mapped out on my mini gardening diagram.

During formation, this diagram has more drafts than any other piece I have ever written. I move things around and try to decide where to put the tomatoes and the peppers and wouldn't the little patch of Johnny Jump-Ups look great by the garden?

"No." Okay. I'll put them in the sidewalk boxes.

The diagramming process hopefully occurs before you start ordering seeds, of course, but I always find myself rearranging up until the very last moment. I'm so wishy-washy sometimes.

Anyway, I plop each tender seedling into its predetermined place and then, the only thing to do is wait, water, weed and protect, if I need to.

Of course, in Denver, I always need to. I have been surprised by more chilly June days and early September snowstorms than anyone should be.

But now it's July, and only the sun inhabits the sky. The temperature has leveled off in the high eighties and low nineties with occasional forays up to 100. Nights are cool by comparison, falling down to the seventies. It's going to get a bit hotter in the dog days of August, but soon, soon will come the harvest and all of my hard work will be rewarded with sweet warm cherry tomatoes eaten straight off the vine, fresh chili rellenos, and buckets of pesto from our special little basil patch!

It's time for me to get to doing what little work I have to do now though. After I finish my tea, I'll saunter out to my little garden areas, weed, and soak the whole bunch with water. Just keep remembering Lesbian Law #1: "Never Underestimate the Power of a Lesbian

Housewyfe."

I can create life, even without a man.

Except maybe the guys from the seed catalogs.

And Jim from next door who gave me some great dirt.

Okay, maybe not.

MAKE YOUR OWN DIRT

My sweet honey-bunny brought the recipe for this classic Southern dessert back from a trip to Texas. She can memorize recipes at the drop of a pot lid. I've always been amazed by that.

And what could be a more suitable snack after a hard day of gardening?

1 large package of cream-filled chocolate cookies
1 cup heavy whipping cream
1 8oz package cream cheese, softened
1 cup powdered sugar
1/2 cup (1 stick) butter, softened
2 cups whole milk
1 3oz box vanilla pudding
1 teaspoon vanilla

Crush cookies. Use a mixer to whip cream into stiff peaks. Combine cream cheese, powdered sugar and butter. Fold whipped cream into cream cheese mixture. In a separate bowl, combine pudding, milk, and vanilla. Beat this mixture until it's the consistency of pudding. Combine both mixtures. Create layers of pudding and crushed cookies in a flower pot, starting with pudding and ending with a thick layer of cookies. Refrigerate until serving time.

My sweet honey-bunny's favorite way to serve this dish is in an opaque flower pot with a sprig of mint stuck into the top. She'll set it in the middle of a table full of people and announce, "Dessert!" Everyone begins to slump into their chairs, eying the pot suspiciously. Then, she plucks the mint out of the middle and chomps it down.

"Mmm." People begin to panic.

I appear with the bowls and a big ladle and save the day. I don't know if it is the surprise or the actual dessert that everybody loves but the entire party tends to go home very satisfied.

·♥·♥·♥·♥·♥·

INDEPENDENCE DAY

This year, on our way home from our vacation, we stayed a while in Evanston, Wyoming to purchase fireworks. I hadn't been in a fireworks store or even at a fireworks stand since I was in high school—maybe even elementary school.

Even then, I had never seen anything like this.

Cool and smelling of sulphur, the firework store's concrete floors and bare metal shelving reminded me of a warehouse. Shelves with stacked palettes filled with shrink-wrapped fireworks lined the sides and center of the large room. Firecrackers, bottle rockets, roman candles, and fountains with names like Delirium and Patriotic Fantasy decked these halls. Everything from sparklers to artillery shells shone in bright boxes promising wilder colors, higher loft and louder bangs.

My sweet honey-bunny's eyes widened and her breathing became shallow as she entered her nirvana. "Okay, let's check it out," she said in a husky voice.

Uh-oh. I knew she liked fireworks, but I never actually realized how much she gave up for our Tux.

My parents called him "the granddog" even though he officially belonged to my mother-in-law. For most of his life, she lived with us, so his pack consisted of we three ladies and him. He was the leader, of course. Cats, visitor dogs, and close friends formed his peripheral world, and we often met people on the street who called us merely, "Tux's mom."

A black and white border collie bred on the Front Range of Colorado, Tux was tall, long and lanky for cattle herding. He came to live with us in the fall of 1993. Already a year old and full of spunk, he caught me with his eyes as I was checking out at the Petsmart one Saturday afternoon. Deep and brown, that liquid look caught my heart and pulled it right into his chest. By the time I arrived back home, I knew I was going back.

Barb, my mother-in-law, walked every day, and always asked us to come with her, but my sweet honey-bunny and I worked constantly and never had the time. Suddenly, the dog with the big brown eyes looked like the solution to a problem.

Miracle dog! Walk with Barb!

I discussed the idea with my sweet honey-bunny, who agreed quickly, and bundled Barb into the car to meet her destiny.

Back at the store, I pushed Barb into the little glass fronted room where he was caged and left her there to fall in love. I spoke to the kind people from the Denver Dumb Friends League and set up the deal, answering questions correctly and filling out the paperwork. The woman informed me that the dog was going a bit stir crazy, so if Barb wanted to walk him around the store carefully and get acquainted, she needed to make sure he didn't get too aggressive with other dogs. Apparently, he was beginning to get a bit violent due to the close quarters. One borrowed leash, and they were off to tour the store.

I bought supplies and by the time we all arrived back at the desk (without a single aggressive doggie incident) to pay the adoption fee, I was a few dollars short. The kind woman just took the difference out of the donation bucket and offered us the use of the leash for our trip home. Apparently, due to that stir craziness, this dog only had one more day left to be adopted, or he'd need to be put down. I stifled my pride, took the cash and leash, and promised I would return the next day with both.

Which I did.

On the way home, the dog stationed himself in the floorboards under Barb's feet and stared at her. She named him Tuxedo Junction.

Tux was one of those dogs who was "the best dog."

Despite the warnings from the well-meaning volunteer, Tux befriended many dogs. He even taught other dogs how to be good dogs like him. One stupid Pekinese mix needed to learn how to use the dog door every time she visited. A roommate's puppy discovered that dogs only poop outside with his guidance.

A neighbor once stopped me on the way to the car to thank us. She said that if it hadn't been for Tux, she never could have trained her new pug puppy to come. As soon as he saw Tux follow the command, the puppy came every time.

Very early in our ownership of this pup, Tux shared an apple with my sweet honey-bunny's baby cousin, Jacob. Jacob sat on our hardwood floor clad in a baby tee and his diaper. His wobbly hand held his apple. One bite for him and then he held the apple out toward Tux. Tux took a little nibble, careful to leave the apple in Jacob's hand. They finished the apple in about ten minutes, after which Jacob grabbed Tux's tail for a ride around the living area. We sat with Jacob's mother, amazed and staring, giggling at the temerity of the very young and the patience of this barely two-year-old dog who just the night before had been disciplined for chewing on the furniture.

Tux was afraid of only one thing: loud noises. Every Fourth of July, we covered him with towels and half-closed the door to our closet where he hid.

During one particular thunderstorm, I remember searching for him until our neighbors called. Sneaking into their house, he'd hidden himself in their closet to tremble and wait out the storm. All of my coaxing skills were tested as I pulled him out of their closet during a less thundery part of the rainstorm. At least he could hide in his own closet!

In 2006, sweet smart Tux's body gave out and we had to say good-bye.

My sweet honey-bunny and I each went through our own grieving process. Even five months later, we'd look at each other and say "I miss Tux today" or "you know who that makes me think of" or "I heard that thunder and immediately looked to see where Tux was."

However, in our practical optimism, we have finally found our silver lining for this sad situation. I should amend that lining from silver to sparkly gold, red, green and blue.

Oh yes, the fireworks are coming back to our house.

After Tux's death, my sweet honey-bunny revealed that she loved fireworks and had always denied herself the bliss of exploding things because Tux feared loud noises so much.

Now, certain fireworks are illegal in Colorado and, for the benefit of any peace officers in my audience, I would like to emphasize that we bought nothing that was illegal.

That we have been caught with.

Yet.

We cruised up and down the aisles of that small concrete-lined bunker of a fireworks store in Evanston, first thinking that we could simply carry our purchases in our arms, changing to the little hand basket halfway through the store, and finally graduating to the full sized shopping cart. My sweet honey-bunny picked out roman candles, bottle rockets, fountains and firecrackers while I grabbed sparklers, party poppers, worms, and little fantasy fireworks shaped like chickens and bees.

Being the only ones in the store aside from the two teenage girls working the register (it was only late May at that point), we began asking questions when we arrived at the checkout counter.

"How is this fountain?"

"It's our best one."

"Are these three foot long sparklers really good?"

"They're awesome."

"Are these fireworks the bangiest?"

Bangiest? Did she just say bangiest?

"No. You want the ladyfingers." I watched the taller brunette circle the counter, pluck the firecrackers from my sweet honey-bunny's hand and deftly snatch the other packet from the cart, ending up with both held between two fingers in a most disapproving grasp.

Wow. I guess they really weren't the bangiest.

Brunette girl tilted her head in the direction of the firecrackers and led my sweet honey-bunny away while I stayed to oversee her redhaired compatriot ring in our purchases. At the firecracker shelf, brunette girl tossed the rejects back into their place and picked up the infamous ladyfingers. "Three of these will blow up a toilet."

"Really."

"And they work underwater."

They must have extra security in the bathrooms at the Evanston, Wyoming school district.

My sweet honey-bunny grabbed two packets and headed back to the front as quickly as she could without feeling she was losing coolness points with either of the teenagers running the place.

We spent $191.62 on fireworks.

In my sweet honey-bunny's defense, it had been over a decade.

In my defense, it was "buy one, get one free" on everything in the store.

I'm quite the bargain hunter.

So, this year, following the municipal firework display, we scooted down to the elementary school near our house with my sweet honey-bunny's now 12 year old cousin Jacob in tow and set off quite a few fireworks. They buzzed and popped and whizzed and fizzed. They flew far into the air and exploded with trails of hot ash floating behind. They flared and fountained.

Meanwhile, this young fellow's face glowed with happiness in the brief flashes of light as he learned how to correctly ignite fuses with a punk from a forty-seven year old woman coming back into her own.

For myself, I take solace in the flashes of light, the smell of sulphur, and the smile on my sweet honey-bunny's face. One day we might own another dog.

But not for a long, long time.

My sweet honey-bunny stocked up.

Firework Safety for Pyromaniacs

Around the holidays, my sweet honey-bunny begins to pull out her fireworks and call her little friends. Her love of fireworks includes passing the love along, and that means teaching children (at least 10 years old) about fireworks.

One of the things I have noticed about this process is that these children learn patience along with firework safety. What a lesson! And so hard to learn. I remember one year, standing in the absolutely below freezing cold watching a young man holding a lighted punk to the fuse of a particularly recalcitrant cone and saying "Mom, it won't light! I need a match. I can't get it to light."

His mother looked at my sweet honey-bunny and laughed, and they both said "Just get closer with the punk. Use the orange part!" He followed their sage advice and soon we had a cone of jumping multicolored sparks.

Patience is the biggest part of learning about firework safety – and most other techniques to safely deal with dangerous things. I don't think there's been a person yet who has been hurt or gotten something terribly wrong or caused someone else injury because they took the time to set up safety precautions while working with fireworks.

My sweet honey-bunny definitely sets her stage well. We start with picking the location. Luckily, our driveway is paved, as is our next door neighbors', so we have a great place to play.

Next, the safety precautions come out. A hose with the sprayer attachment is primed and at the ready. A bucket of water and aluminum roasting pan of sand join that device. The long pipe that my sweet honey-bunny rigged to plunge into the lawn for bottle rockets and roman candles gets set up. Punks are lit and placed in a suitable container which won't tip over easily.

Now, time for fireworks. Bring out the box and start the festivities! On the rare occasions where a dud occurs, leave it alone and stay out of its area for at least twenty minutes. Then, spray it with water (a fun job for the designated hose-holder) and dump it into the bucket of water to get completely soaked and destroyed.

If, after the fun has ceased its banging and clanging and whooping and zinging, we have any fireworks left over, we store them in a cool, dark place where little prying eyes and fingers can't get to them. I always try to make sure that nothing is left over so that I can participate in my favorite part of the firework process.

Shopping!

A great resource is the National Safety Council. Their helpful website gives great tips and includes a video about firework safety. I mean, if my parents had made me watch a video on firework safety on July 3rd, I definitely would have thought they were lame, but at least they'd know I had that knowledge under my belt and that's more important (and potentially less expensive) than being cool in the eyes of your children.

Or maybe I'm just cheap and don't want to spend money on doctors.

I have been known to search out a sale or two in my life.

And not just on fireworks, either.

·♥·♥·♥·♥·♥·

THE GUIDE TO SURVIVING SPORTING EVENTS

At the tender age of nine, in a futile attempt to fit in with my classmates, I begged and pestered my poor parents until they agreed to trot me down to the old ball field and sign me up for softball. They spent the remainder of their summer dragging me to practice.

This experience provided all of us with the sure and steadfast knowledge that the only danger I presented to the other team was the chance that a fly ball would smack me on the head and cause a game delay while the medical team scraped me off the ground.

My only athletic talent seemed the mysterious ability to become distracted by inanimate objects while actually playing the game. After realizing that my current state of athleticism was not about to change, the dedicated coaches of my softball team stopped telling me where the games were.

I believe that my parents were in collusion with them.

This was just my first sign from God that I was not meant for great athletic feats. In future years, I found myself failing physical education exams, getting kicked out of gymnastics class, and breaking my hand while playing a game of intramural broomball. For those of you without knowledge of this particular sport, just imagine a bunch of college students running around on ice pretending they are playing hockey with brooms for sticks, a kid's inflatable ball for a puck, and sneakers substituting for skates. They promised me that it wasn't like real sports.

Liars!

My complete athletic experience has been spent on the bench worrying that the coach was going to make me play, in the game completely terrorized that someone was going to hit the ball my way, or back on the bench in total pain because I attempted to play the game. As soon as I realized this, I ended my athletic career.

Can you really end something which never got started?

Having said all this, I believe that I can honestly utter the phrase, "I am not a jock."

Therefore, I went and got married to someone who was. I still can't figure out how that happened.

Due to her full-body embrace of athleticism, I found myself once again immersed in the bosom of the great lesbian community: the softball field.

Lesbian Law #23: "Each lesbian must attend a minimum of two dozen softball games in her lifetime. At least one half of these must be in adulthood."

Oh yes, if you won't go willingly, you will end up dating or even marrying someone who will drag you to them. It's just God's little way of saying "Gotcha!"

I was lucky. My wyfe finally left that softball team. Even though this was not my goal, the side effects are great! I haven't been forced onto a field in years. I feel blessed.

However, although I have an understandable aversion to playing sports, I find that I very much enjoy watching others play.

Yes, even the Lesbian Housewyfe has been bitten by the Extreme

Olympic Horsy Tennis Bug. You probably have friends who have succumbed as well. In my case, I am glued to the television for about three to four weeks out of each year. My events are the Extreme or X-Games, the Olympics (winter and summer), all the Grand Slam tennis tournaments I can find on TV, and anything with a horse involved—including rodeos.

The Olympics are pretty self-explanatory, as are the tennis tournaments (I still haven't figured out the scoring yet), and any girl who ever loved horses understands the last. Now the hard one.

The Extreme Games were first shown on ESPN in 1995 and I was hooked. These people jump out of airplanes on surfboards, climb steep manufactured mountains, and fling themselves around on bicycles, skateboards, and in-line skates. The most impressive of these crazy folk trek across miles of wilderness in a sport called Adventure Racing. This year, one of the members of the winning team popped a tendon in her knee on the next to last day of the race and still finished. And she was one of the oldest people at the games. Nothin' but butch there.

I find that my fascination with sports grows each time a new event begins. I'm one of those people who sits with a box of kleenex at her elbow and teary eyes glued to the television screen. I sob with the excellence of it all.

Sometimes my friends will watch with me and try to berate the dedicated young athletes because they didn't do something as well as the guy from Sweden. My only response is, "Could you do that?" They respectfully clam up.

Strangely enough, I find that my loyalty is exclusively to those athletes whose names are forgotten after the games end. I could care less about Michael Jordan or John Elway. Maybe that has to do with the idea that they have enough fans.

But I digress....

Not even I wish to admit that all I did all day is sit around and watch television, although it has happened more than once. "Sports Fever" can capture your attention in a way that no other entertainment can. And you can't videotape it because then the excitement will be lost. Unfortunately, you still have a job to do.

Fortunately, I have an answer. (As if I'd be writing about this if I didn't) The only way to survive this "Sports Fever" and still maintain your housewifely status is to pick the right chores to perform and carefully schedule them. I have found a line of chores which I call the "Do Practically Nothing" or DPN chores. These chores require a minimum of effort and create a full day of work.

The best "Do Practically Nothing" chore is laundry. All you do is dump your laundry items into the washer, sorting as you go (after all, you only have a three to five minute commercial break), and let the machines do all the work while you sit back and watch cute little Miss Steffi Graf slam another one away.

When your wonderful supportive wyfe comes home after a hard day on the job and asks what you did today, you can look her straight in the eye and exclaim (completely guilt-free), "Laundry." I don't know anyone who doesn't fold the clothes in front of the television anyway, so there we go.

Thank God for the person who invented the washing machine! Where would I be without it? Out in a stream somewhere scrubbing clothes against rocks.

Ick.

Laundry can be complicated, however, by the introduction into your life of Lesbian Law #18: "Conserve all energy except yours." In this case, one must adhere to one's time schedule with a vengeance unseen outside of the German train system.

As soon as the commercial break starts, run back to the washer and empty it. Collect any stray clothespins you will need, as if time allows. Then, at the next break, trudge out to the clothesline and hang your clothes quickly, quickly, quickly! A kitchen timer is always useful in this situation. I did this for a couple of years before insisting on the installation of a dryer. Who wants to hang their clothes outside in the middle of winter anyhow?

If you have a dishwasher, dishes can be handled in the same way. Very cool.

Even if you are washing dishes by hand, just let them air-dry. There is never a need to dry your dishes with a towel unless you really need that cup NOW. And don't let anyone tell you different.

Another good DPN chore is baking. However, schedule this task during one of the events you don't particularly care about like hockey or any of the Dream Team's basketball games. I find splitting prep time into three to five minute intervals affects your final product in a very detrimental way. However, once you get into the rising and baking stages, you're home free! Can you tell that my personal favorite in the baking department is bread?

Baking bread is my therapy. I can recommend nothing sweeter to solve a marital spat than slamming some dough onto a counter and beating it up for eight minutes. Then the yeasty smell of rising and baking bread fills the house. You take out a stick of butter as soon as you start the first rise and, by the time the bread leaves the oven, you have the perfect consistency to coat each warm slice.

Your spouse is guaranteed to show up willing to apologize (whether or not they really did anything wrong) when you pull that hot loaf out of the oven. With all of your anger spent in the kneading process, you may simply smile, slice the bread, and accept these heartfelt apologies.

Plus, you have enjoyed two to three hours of watching the cute little women's gymnastics team bound about on mats and bars and other weird equipment that just make you think "Ouch." Have a second slice, you busy bee! You've already burned up those calories.

As you can see, the main characteristics of "Do Practically Nothing" chores are that they take a maximum of three to five minutes to get started and a minimum of effort to sustain. Any chore which can follow these stringent guidelines qualifies! But good scheduling is intrinsic. One slip up and you might miss the synchronized swimming or the mass street luge. No one wants that to happen.

After that, all you need to add is your imagination. Who else do you know who can go to a fancy dinner and be doing their laundry simultaneously?

These chores are magic!

So I send you out into the world to enjoy the fruits of my wisdom. Use these tools sparingly, my children. They are powerful and other's knowledge can mar the admiration of those around you. Remember Lesbian Law #1: "Never underestimate the power of a Lesbian Housewyfe."

We "non-jocks" have got to stick together.

Do Practically Nothing Chores

These quick and easy chores can all be handily split up into sections or completed in three to five minutes. I've also included a few which can be completed in front of the television as you watch, with short moments when you absolutely must leave the room.

Laundry: Unless you are obsessive in your stain treatment, throwing a load of laundry into the machine or transferring it to your dryer will only take three to five minutes. Once the laundry is dry, pile the clothes into your basket and take it into the television room to be folded. Putting the laundry away can be done during the commercials. However, if you are obsessive about your sports like me, you'll want a television in the kitchen and bedroom as well so you won't miss a thing.

Changing the Linens: A big part of my laundry process is switching out the towels and sheets. I keep a clean supply on hand so I can whip through the bathroom, pulling towels off the racks and resupplying within my given commercial break. For the sheets, I break the chore into separate bits. One commercial break, I remove the sheets and throw them into the pile for the laundry. Next commercial break, I put the fitted bottom sheet on the bed. Next one, the flat sheet and pillowcases. Isn't it funny how making the bed always takes longer than breaking it down? Just like everything else I suppose.

Baking: Baking has to be planned out quite distinctly. Bread must be started in advance with your first kneading process rigidly scheduled before your program actually begins. Then, the rising takes care of itself. Punching down and shaping your loaves takes only moments, as does slipping the loaves in and out of the oven.

Cookies can be quickly mixed up, and their ten to twelve minute baking time provides an ample space in which to finish up that race or game. However, don't pick filled cookies or anything finicky like that. A simple chocolate chip or sugar cookie fills the bill amply.

Cakes and pies are pretty much impossible unless you have a television in the kitchen. I think they just require too much time in blocks.

Sorting Magazines: I have way too many magazines. Really. I collect certain ones (Martha Stewart Living, Cook's Illustrated, Crochet) and then others I just receive, read intensively and recycle after storing the appropriate recipes, patterns or interesting articles. This means that once every month, I have to go through my magazine rack and sort through the mass. With this tiny bit of work, I create a feeling of accomplishment, carrying the mounds of magazines to be recycled out to the bin. I always do this in front of the television and do all my toting during commercials.

Exercising: A fabulous friend of mine, Linda Buch, wrote a groundbreaking book: *The Commercial Break Workout*. Oh yes. She created workout routines for during commercial breaks and even some for during the shows. It's like she read my mind. I pull this book out when I'm feeling particularly recalcitrant about going outside to get a great workout without missing my programs. I love it!

·❤·❤·❤·❤·❤·

PLAYING BALL

My mother looked across the formica countertop. "Softball. You want to play softball." She sighed with resignation, and continued to chop the carrot.

"Everybody else is trying out!" I persisted, meaning the cool girls, the jocks, the ones who left me in the line until a teacher made someone pick me. I stood there patiently, embarrassed and not wanting to play anyway. Kickball, dodgeball, and volleyball all meant the same thing to me.

Pain.

Pain in my side from dodgeball, pain in my toes from kickball, pain on my wrists from volleyball. Swelling and bruising and broken blood vessels etching their way across my white inner arms. Standing on the volleyball court praying that no one would strike the weakest link in the chain.

That would be me.

The smallest, weakest, and, if I had already been playing some sort of ball game, injured. Of course, I was book-smart, but that doesn't count on the playing field. I understood the rules of the game. I understood that you had to play a sport to get some respect, and maybe some friendship, from the cool girls.

Unfortunately, that understanding did nothing to improve my

hand/eye coordination.

So, there I was, terrified of balls (a condition that persists to this day) and desperate to be cool, pleading with my mother to allow me to play softball. Looking back, I can only imagine what went through her mind at that moment.

We never had enough money, and this would mean a uniform fee and a team fee, along with tennis shoes and baseball gloves. Driving me around the Arkansas summer in our unairconditioned car, bats and balls and glove scattered across the backseat with my younger brother. The inevitable fight for "who gets the front seat" each time we entered the car. (The term "shotgun" was not permitted in our pacifist household.) Sullen trips home after my team lost and sniffles if I didn't get to play.

Sporty greatness was beyond my imagination, but maybe I could at least be good at it. Who knew? Perhaps my latent talent for softball just needed to be tapped! This could turn out to be my "thing." So much better than singing in church (lame!), or reading at an elevated level (You think you're so smart—Lame!), or writing poetry (Super-Fruity Lame!).

Maybe God would let me be good at softball.

I could throw a baseball. Dad and I played catch occasionally and I could always hit his hand. (Though now I suspect that he moved to catch rather than me hitting the target on my own.) Softball had potential. Plus, if the ball hit me, it wouldn't hurt that bad, right? Soft. Ball.

My mother relented and drove me to sign up and get my t-shirt. She grabbed the practice and game schedule and planned my summer.

I've heard that war consists of long periods of boredom interspersed with quick moments of sheer terror. My entire softball experience can be summed up with the same words.

And yet, I played. I practiced and went to games and stood in left (or was it right?) field like a good least valuable player, trying my darnedest to catch or retrieve and throw that ball back to the infield. More often than not, the ball bounced off my outstretched glove while I flinched at the surprise of impact. Time to retrieve!

Were my eyes closed at the time? Of course! Can anyone can catch one of those things with their eyes open?!

Out of pity for the other players, my coach placed me where I could do the least damage.

In right (or was it left?) field, I contemplated the dandelions and the grass or watched the stands or just stared at the bench, wishing I could sit down. My book and my fellow players were there and that meant reading and cheering. In left (or was it right?) field, I never cheered. Cheering reminded people I was there. If I stayed quiet, they would forget I existed. Maybe then, no one would hit the ball at me.

The last time I remember playing softball as a child, I had decided that catcher would be the perfect position. The pitcher threw the ball, the bat swung and if the player missed, the ball came across the plate the same way every time. Easy-peasy catches every time!

Out in right (or left?) field, the ball zoomed at me from all over the place. If I happened to catch sight of it, my little legs ran as fast as they could take me (which wasn't very fast) to get there in time for the ball to bounce off my glove. Then, holding the retrieved ball, I would run back towards the infield, only stopping when I was sure I could huck that sucker far enough to reach second base. The coach instructed me to throw to second base. And, as a good girl, second base always received that ball.

Most of the time from just a few feet away.

Anyway, there I was between the batter and umpire, amazed at how far away the pitcher was placed and how far behind the batter I had to be. After hearing that bat whiff over my head once, I moved back a little further. The umpire caught the first six pitches, and then began to attempt to teach me how to catch. Sure that I had actually found my calling, I was determined to catch the next one. Here came the pitch and I lined up on it with my glove outstretched in front of my face. The bat whiffed and, as had happened so many times before, I miscalculated. The ball whizzed by my glove and whacked me right in the face. I went down like a sack of sand.

Soft ball. A soft ball is the head of a dandelion gone to seed. A soft ball is a wad of cotton used to clean your face. A soft ball is the perfect stage to add the pecans and vanilla to your pralines. A softball is not a soft ball, and when a softball knocks you out, that's when you have to take it like the smallest, weakest girl on the team and call it quits.

Without consulting me, my parents stopped ferrying me to practice and softball magically disappeared. Later, one of the cool girls taunted me with the truth, that the team had stopped telling me where the games were. I was embarrassed, but realized something important. Freedom from a horrible nightmare brings relief with only a tinge of guilt. It's hard to say I'm not strong or fast or brave enough, but after you wake up on your back staring at a hot blue sky, pick yourself up, drag your black eye over to your mother, and cry all the way home, you find the words pretty easily.

Only love explains why I am now standing in the pouring rain behind home plate once again. Without even considering the impact of softball in my life, I went and got married to someone who was a jock. I still can't figure out how that happened. Due to her full-body embrace of athleticism, I found myself once again immersed in the bosom of the great lesbian community: the softball field. Lesbian Law #23: "Each lesbian must attend a minimum of two dozen softball games in her lifetime. At least one half of these must be in adulthood."

Oh yes, if you won't go willingly, you will end up dating or even marrying someone who will drag you to them. It's just God's little way of saying "Gotcha!"

As for my current plight, the umpire yells out "Strike Two!" and both the batter and I look at him with a silent plea. Call this game. Please call this game. We're all soaked, the rain isn't letting up, and the ball is now officially impossible for even the good players to catch. He nods for us to play on and I throw the ball back out to the pitcher who has come halfway from the mound so she can catch it.

I throw like the wretched little non-jock I am.

They needed a girl today on this co-ed community team, which is why I'm playing at all. We arrived at the field to the news that the team was one girl short. If I didn't play, the team would automatically lose. They looked at me like if I played, that might change the outcome. I stared back, knowing their predicament and having no pity, ready to head off to the bar, my favorite part of the softball game. Didn't they remember the last time I played? Or did they just not care if they won or lost, only that they got to play the game?

Then, Stephanie's eyes met mine and I knew I couldn't let her down.

"You don't have to...." She said, with a plea in her eyes.

"Right." I replied, and held my hand out for a glove.

"Okay!" The team captain leaped over to the umpire to let him know we were all here and ready to play.

They told me where to go and there I stood, sullen, sure that all of this was a terrible mistake. I was in the catcher's position. I guess everyone remembered the never-ending innings from the last time I played, balls whizzing by me in left (or was it right?) field once the other team realized I couldn't catch. More dodgeball than softball.

When the rain began to drizzle out of the sky, I was sure I was free, but the umpire doggedly held his ground until lightning zinged across the sky.

Never before and never since have I seen such a beautiful bolt of electricity.

I turned to the umpire. He sighed and pushed back his mask. "All right," he relented, and called the game.

That was the last softball game I played.

There are ways to avoid actual sweat and still stay in your wyfe's good graces. For instance, you can temporarily revoke Lesbian Law #22: "Everyone gets a chance to play" in the middle of, well, any game, thereby insuring a victory for your team and a little bit of relaxation for you. This strategy lacks any sort of guarantee, though. Unfortunately, most lesbians respond to this generous offer by saying, "It doesn't matter if we win or lose. You just go have fun" (which is, actually, Lesbian Law #32). They don't realize that if you never entered a playing field in your entire lifetime, it wouldn't be long enough between games. Therefore, I am passing on the fruits of my wisdom, also known as:

LA's Femme Tips for Surviving Sports.

Tip #1: Always wear a dress and heels when attending any sporting event. You'll look and feel great and, in the event that the softball team doesn't have enough women, there is no way that you can play.

Tip #2: Lesbian Law #21: "The duty of the femme at sporting events is to bring the refreshments." Good cookies and a special knack for margaritas are always a socially acceptable substitute for actually participating in any game. The margaritas just need enough tequila for the rest of your teammates to forget you're there.

Tip #3: An enthusiastic cheerleader is worth three good infielders. If you can get your teammates to believe this, you are officially home free.

Remember Lesbian Law #1: "Never underestimate the power of a Lesbian Housewyfe."

I make great cookies.

Originally published in Out Front Magazine

"YOU CAN'T MAKE ME" OATMEAL CHOCOLATE CHIP COOKIES

Cookies might be the most perfect picnic food. Completely self-contained and filling, these filling and almost healthy cookies satisfy most appetites and give much needed energy for the trip to the bar following the softball game.

1 cup butter
1 cup brown sugar
1/2 cup sugar
2 eggs
1 teaspoon vanilla
1 1/2 cup flour
1 teaspoon baking soda
1 teaspoon cinnamon
1/2 teaspoon salt
1/8 teaspoon nutmeg
3 cups of oats
1 cup semisweet chocolate chips
1/2 cup white chocolate chips

Cream together the butter and sugars. Add eggs, one at a time. Add vanilla. Sift together dry ingredients and slowly add that mixture to the butter. Stir in the oats, adding more if necessary to create a very, very, very stiff batter. Stuff those oats in there! Add the chocolate chips. Drop by rounded teaspoons onto ungreased cookie sheets and bake 10-15 minutes in a 350 degree oven. Cool one minute on the cookie sheet and remove to wire racks or a cut-open and laid flat brown paper bag (That's what I usually do - Lesbian Law #2: "Reduce, reuse, recycle."). Cool completely, stealing only one or two while warm. Store in an airtight container.

I've also frozen these cookies before baking so I can pull out a few at a time for parties or just dessert. Use the same baking instructions and you have fresh, warm, melty chocolate dessert. Yummy!

·♥·♥·♥·♥·♥·

WHEN ICONS COLLIDE

I love popular culture. Well, really, by definition, everybody loves popular culture. I mean, otherwise it wouldn't be popular, would it? Like June Cleaver, some of us are destined to become a part of popular culture. Like me, some of us are destined to just enjoy it. Pop culture happenings tend to be taken very seriously while they are occurring and, afterward, turn to total cheesiness. This is when I can get down to business.

Finally, for example, I am able to enjoy the O.J. Simpson trial. Before it ended, one had to have an opinion and, being that I am the Lesbian Housewyfe, the expectation of a high O.J.Q. loomed always. Plus, Lesbian Law #5 is "I will always be loudly and vociferously involved with any political or high profile action having any impact, big or small, on the lives of women around the world even if I don't know what it's all about."

Although I am in constant contact with my television, I knew less than most people about the trial and, frankly, worked to keep it that way. Past popular culture has always fascinated me more and my afternoon mysteries are too good to miss! I just discovered *Charlie's Angels*, a show just bursting with cheesiosity that I missed the first time around. My mother refused to have it on in the house; it was too sexist and violent. She was right of course, but now I love it so! And not just

Charlie's Angels, those convoluted plot lines of *Banacek* and *Columbo* keep me coming back for more. And the slick way they recycled plots from *MacMillan and Wife* for *Hart to Hart*. The mind boggles.

Plus, those hairdos. I envy those Farrah wings. My hair would never do that. Now, of course, I follow Lesbian Law #10 which is "Naturalness is the key to true beauty." Most of the time, a simple ponytail holder is enough, but when I'm in the midst of it all, I still want that poufy do of Stephanie Powers. But, no matter how much I laugh, in reruns, they are still making money off of it.

Not as much as Mr. O.J. Simpson though. Now that this chapter in our immediate pop culture has ended (really, let it go. It's time for the whole matter to fade away), lots of funny facts are surfacing. For example, O.J. made more money in jail than out. He has made the nightly news nationally every night for over a year. Before the trial, he couldn't pay to get mentioned except on sports networks or, on the extreme occasion, Entertainment Tonight. Now, everyone wants to see O.J., or better yet, have a piece of O.J. A signature, a picture, a copy of the book. We were in a mass hysteria-just like when we all had that famous Farrah do, just like when the hostages were released from Iran. Except this was bigger.

At 11AM mountain standard time on October 3, 1995, traffic stopped. Phones ceased their ringing in busy offices. College professors wheeled televisions into the classroom and struggled with the vertical hold. I turned the television on, sat down, and stopped folding clothes. We all waited breathlessly for the verdict. All but one.

Steamboat Springs, Colorado is a busy resort town. There's great skiing in the winter, I'm told. I don't do sports myself. The Lovely Lesbian Housewyfe is not a jock. Yet, I enjoy myself while I'm in Steamboat.

Anyway, this is where my sister-in-law (as a lesbian, I use the term loosely) lives without a television set. She is, however, nowhere near sheltered from the outside world. She works in a steakhouse which is where one works in a resort town and is exposed to many different opinions regarding popular culture issues. She also lives in a trailer park called "Dream Island" which is where the story of this little lost lamb begins.

On that seemingly insignificant October morning, just after 11, she entered the manager's office to pay her lot fee, a normal monthly occurrence. The woman turned to my sister-in-law and two popular culture icons collided.

"Have you been following the Simpson trial?" The manager asked with breathless excitement.

"I thought the baby shot him," my sister-in-law replied, referring to the previous night's bar topic, a long diatribe from a regular about the results of the ongoing mystery on *The Simpsons*.

O.J. smashed into Bart, Homer, and Maggie with a clash heard now around the world. Sparks of brightly colored animation cells and trial footage burst from the manager's ears as she struggled with the wild concepts. Finally, with a strange sigh of surrender, she looked quizzically at this lovely innocent and said, "He's not guilty."

My sister-in-law recognized the reference.

Ah yes, the great machine slowly, sneakily sucks us all in. But I promise to remain here, holding staunchly to my position of making fun of it all for, as all of you know, Lesbian Law #1 is "Never Underestimate the Power of the Lesbian Housewyfe."

The new icon has arrived.

MUSIC TO KEEP YOU CLEANIN'

I've got to clean my house, and that process needs a soundtrack. Something to keep my feet moving. Something to keep my butt off the couch. Something to keep me dusting and scrubbing and sweeping and mopping and moving, moving, moving.

Enjoy these pop-forward tunes!

Housework – Robert Palmer

I Can Cook – Dennis Caiazza & Swing Factory

Angel With An Attitude – The Ditty Bops

Burn Down the House – Shedaisy

Redneck Woman – Gretchen Wilson

Everyday America – Sugarland

No Life Without Wife – Bride & Prejudice Soundtrack

Come On-A My House – Rosemary Clooney

Shopping – Barenaked Ladies

Fish to Fry – The Ditty Bops

God Bless the American Housewife – Shedaisy

The House is Rockin – Stevie Ray Vaughn

Help! – The Beatles

The House That Jack Built – Aretha Franklin

Keep Young and Beautiful – Annie Lennox

Brick House – The Commodores

Barrelhouse Woman – Champion Jack Dupree

Ray's Rockhouse – Manhattan Transfer

Our House – Crosby, Stills, Nash & Young

Nice Work If You Can Get It – Billie Holliday

Still Dirrty – Christina Aguilera

Mission Impossible Theme – U2 version

If those don't keep you going, I don't know what will.

·♥·♥·♥·♥·♥·

CLEANING KARMA

As a young girl, I had a definite picture of how my life would blossom. I saw myself growing up as a jet-setting, horse-riding, freelance-writing detective with a handsome and fabulous husband and a houseboy named Max. I wasn't sure how to make this happen, but I was pretty sure (at the tender age of eight) that the opportunity would just suddenly appear.

My teenage years amended that picture to a more bohemian actress and writer, always wearing a flowing cape like a superhero. Super LA! Fighting crime and small minds across the Ozarks and around the world. My new alter ego uttered wise words which shaped philosophies and tore down mountains of established thought. However, even in my most Communist bohemian dreams, I must have had a housekeeper. That amazing woman with long flowing hair and stylish cape would never stagger out of the bathroom wearing bright yellow rubber gloves.

Yet here I am. Standing over my porcelain throne, I wonder if that goddess even had a toilet in her home. I'm sure the bathroom served only to hold her giant bathtub which she filled with bubbles and surrounded with candles to read the books that she wrote as she relaxed in the perfect temperature water for hours.

My God! I still want her life!

The toilet snarls at me and I brandish my white toilet brush. I'm wearing my standard cleaning outfit, cutoff jean shorts, old college t-shirt, yellow rubber gloves covering my hands and barefoot so my shoes don't track in any additional dirt.

One more time I ask myself, "why are you doing this?" I am forced to answer, "because I am sick of the bathroom of doom that even I, with my history of grimy Arkansas filling station toilets, am nervous about entering."

The pink stain at the water line taunted me. That couldn't be good. I took a deep breath, regretted it, and spurted the cleanser around the inside rim of the beast. Slamming the lid, I sat down and surveyed the rest of the bathroom.

When I was a teenager, I earned my allowance by cleaning the house for my mother. The bathroom and living room plagued me each Saturday morning (or afternoon. I was a teenager after all.). "Start at the top and work down," my mother always said, and that advice I continue to follow to this day. Here's my routine:

Cleanser into the toilet bowl for marinating.

Move every article covering a surface (shampoo, soap, lotions, towels, knick-knacks, magazines, scale) out of the bathroom.

Sweep the floor.

Use glass cleaner on the mirror and wipe it down with newspaper (newspaper makes the glass shine more!).

Scrub out the sink, toilet, shower and/or bathtub with your sponge and some regular bathroom cleanser like Comet. An old toothbrush handily scours the fixtures and finally rinse with either the sponge (after completely rinsing the Comet out) or by filling an old plastic cup from a fast-food stop with water and tossing it to splash down the walls and sides of the tub and shower.

Scrub the toilet with the handy dandy toilet brush.

Mop the floor.

After drying, move knick-knacks, etc. back into their places.

And there we are. One clean bathroom.

The routine sounds simple. I grimace at the thought. At least I've got one step done. I could just scrub the toilet bowl and no one would be the wiser. Then I spot the giant dust bunny under the sink. Crap.

This is my penance for accepting the role of "housewyfe", though I will love the fact that the bathroom is clean. I understand the zen of cleaning. The way corners tuck into place on perfectly made beds makes me smile. Who can resist snuggling into the warm clean laundry fresh from the drier? The lines of the vacuum on the carpet mirror the exquisite lawns across our town. Time to revel in the absolute power of eradicating dirt from my household!

I leap from the toilet and swiftly complete my routine, scrubbing and rubbing and wiping and dusting and mopping and sweeping and tossing and drying. Dirt begone! Outta here, sludge! Weird pink stain va-moose!

Sparkling and smelling of cleanser, the bathroom happily primps. All of my actions today have led to this moment, and I embrace my new alter ego.

After all, don't forget Lesbian Law #1: "Never underestimate the power of the lesbian housewife."

I'm the Queen of the Throne.

READING LIST FOR THE THRONE ROOM

Frankly, I don't do tons of pretense, but I do like to give people something good to read in the bathroom (reading being such an important part of passing the time in a bathroom). Therefore, I recommend a combination of the ridiculous and intellectual. This balance helps keep everyone happy.

Of course, I don't keep all of these reading materials in the bathroom all at the same time. I cycle them in and out as the urge to recycle and postal delivery demands.

People (I call it "*The People*" to my friends, as in "I was reading *The People* and saw that Britiny is on the wagon again.")

Entertainment Weekly

Bon Appetit

Smithsonian

Southern Living

The New Yorker

Cook's Illustrated

Cook's Country

New York Times Book Review

A Book about some project I'm currently endeavoring to complete. During puppy training, <u>Cesar's Way</u> by Cesar Millan and <u>Kathy Santo's Dog Sense</u> could be found there.

Catalogs upon Catalogs upon Catalogs

Harper's Magazine

The New York Times Sunday Magazine

An easy to read book with short essays or lots of colorful pictures. I recommend any of the following:

Anything Can Happen: Notes on My Inadequate Life and Yours by Roger Rosenblatt

Herself: Reflections on a Writing Life by Madeleine L'Engle compiled by Carole F. Chase

Design Like You Give a Damn: Architectural Responses to Humanitarian Crises Edited by Architecture for Humanity

Groovitude: A Get Fuzzy Treasury by Darby Conley

·♥·♥·♥·♥·♥·

CLEARING OUT BEFORE THE FALL

Ahh, spring cleaning. A wonderful tradition dating back to the dawn of mankind. Me? I gave it up years ago. The tradition basically ended with the dawn of womankind. The whole idea gives me the creeps. The lovely Lesbian Housewyfe's relieving factor is, of course, Lesbian Law #20: "Household duties are to be divided equally among all members of the residence unless heavy lifting is involved in which case this particular job falls under the domain of the butchy babe."

Makes me glad to be a June.

Anyway, when spring finally rolls in, I want to open all the windows and let the outdoors in. I garden, I play, I go to the park. I want to be outside! Spring fever hits with a passion unseen since...well, since the previous spring. I don't hold myself back. Chores fall by the wayside. It becomes rare that I enter the house without dirt on the soles of my shoes and under my fingernails. Evil little thoughts scratch their way through my defenses: "It will just get dirty again," "I can blame that on the dog," and "I'm outside slaving in the garden so we can have good food this winter and you want me to clean the house too?!!!"

That last one, when verbalized, may be exchanged for at least one full bathroom cleaning by the unfortunate partner of your choice.

But now, after an entire spring and summer of allowing the outside to unabashadly recline in my living room, guilt overwhelms me and I find that it's time to do the fall cleaning. My sweet honey goes off to face another load of idiot children (I mean students) and I am left at home to face my end of the summer cleaning spree. It always traps me when I am alone and defenseless. After being wrestled to the ground, I cry "UNCLE!" helplessly, continuously regretting the time I spent drinking margaritas and playing in my garden while it was surely lifting weights, preparing for this moment.

What was I thinking?!

My method in the pursuit of cleanliness has three different stages. The first stage I see as a warming up period, making that slow move from gardening lush to busy housewyfe. I call it "Piddling."

Piddling is sort of like extended doodling. One is piddling when one wanders about the house giving too much time to many little things that you need to get done and you're feeling kind of lazy 'cause summer slacker activities do tend to take it out of you and you end up taking two weeks to finish a closet but you have lots of fun doing it.

I am the champion of piddlers. My mother is a piddler as was her mother before her. We are a proud people.

The Piddler stage usually takes the majority of the fall cleaning time. My piddling stage is now at its sixth week. My mother-in-law who lives with us (this is a whole other story) has gone through a variety of fall flower arrangements. My sweet Stephie is in full swing with her little kidlets (midterms, y'know). I have organized the CD's, the videos, all the bathroom literature in the household (Martha Stewart and design magazines go into a file and everything else is recycled) and the pantry. I even found room for all my jellies, or rather, syrups, that I canned. The plants are in and in place and our bedroom closet has been stripped of summer clothes.

Activities like these will probably continue until just before

Thanksgiving when we enter the "Panic 'Cause the Family will be Here in a Week" stage. Family, by the way, being defined under Lesbian Law #5: "Your true family is chosen." Remember, there are exceptions to every law. Mine is my embarrassing Uncle Hubert who I came out to in full regalia during his church's monthly potluck supper. Have you ever noticed that churchgoers and lesbians have certain things in common? But I digress....

The house turns completely upside down with deep cleaning. We work from the top down starting with the cobwebs on the ceiling and ending with a generous swabbing of all the hardwood floors. In between, we vacuum rugs, dust mantles, wash windows, launder furniture coverings, and deep clean everything that isn't nailed down or is nailed down and helplessly exposed.

The whole thing coagulates just as old Aunt Janine walks through the door on the day before Thanksgiving. She shows up early because she wants to "help." We set her to making holiday decorations and tell her that her duty is really to entertain. She believes us and slurps down another glass of wine.

After everything has been thoroughly cleaned, it's time for the third and final step, "Decorating." Since we started cleaning in the fall, we get to start our decorating just in time for Christmas!!!!

That's right.

I am a Christmas-aholic.

I have it under control. I don't start up the Christmas music until after the appearance of Santa Claus in the Macy's Thanksgiving Day Parade. Fortunately, one can pull together the decor before then. Everything has to be ready for Thanksgiving Dinner. This really is my favorite time of year.

As a slightly nontraditional preachers' daughter, I start by decorating for Advent, the time in which Christians prepare for the birth of

Christ. I would like to say that my spirit feeds on that connection with the past but the real truth is I love purple and gold candles.

That's right! One uses purple, pink, white, and gold in decorating for Advent. What a great excuse this makes, especially with my discovery of Lesbian Law #6: "Celebrate diversity in all its forms."

Since the general look is most important to me at this point, I also add silver and green and a subtle touch of deep red.

My favorite decoration for Thanksgiving is my Advent Wreath which takes prominence on the dining table. Advent wreathes, for those of you who don't know, are a circle of three purple candles and one pink candle, symbolizing the apostles, surrounding one tall white candle, the Christ Candle, which must rise above the rest. I'm always a little early but I do love it so, and it gives me a great excuse to avoid dead leaves and those mutant ceramic pilgrims who are always out of proportion with the little plaster turkey.

Frankly, I just say no to that brown and orange color scheme. (Can you believe that seventies orange trend is coming back? God help us! No wonder there are so many suicides over the holidays.)

A traditional wreath graces the front door. Further decorations are introduced after Thanksgiving Day but we won't go into those yet except to say that reindeer and a strange little Christmas tree made entirely of vacuum tubes, Christmas lights, and an inverted terracotta pot with rick-rack around the edge are definitely involved.

In total, my fall cleanup takes about three months, starting with Labor Day and ending at Thanksgiving. Party season begins officially on that sweet November Thursday. So, start your engines and open those broom closets!

And remember Lesbian Law #1: Never Underestimate the Power of a Lesbian Housewyfe.

But first, sit down and enjoy a cup of hot cider.

Energizing Juice Seltzers

Simple to make and sip, these easy drinks rejuvenate me and keep me cleaning for hours. They almost make themselves!

    Juice of your choice
    Seltzer or bubbly mineral water

    Mix 1 part juice to 3 parts seltzer in a tall glass.

·♥ · ♥ · ♥ · ♥ · ♥ ·

AND I RESOLVE TO CLEAN UP MY ACT

E arlier this month, I went up into the attic to find some yarn. While waiting for more yarn to be delivered for a "We're Moving In Together" afghan for my friend Ally's brand new engagement, I decided to use the time to remind myself how to knit. As I looked through the seven paper bags and single plastic garbage bag full of my yarn stash sitting on top of piles of magazines, I realized that I desperately needed to pursue one of my New Years resolutions.

This weekend, I must begin organizing our loft.

Our life in this house began so innocently. We made the decision to move to the new house and organize our stuff as we unpacked each box. Brilliant! I tossed only the obvious as I packed the plethora of boxes, knowing that we would recycle/trash/donate the less obvious choices when unpacking. By the end of the month after arriving in the house, everything would be in its place and there would be a place for everything. Then we could move everything from the storage unit into the house and get rid of that as well! Oooh, the dreams I dreamed.

At the end of our first month in the house, as we sat in the den watching the television perched atop a trio of unpacked boxes, I contemplated the demise of my masterful plan. Boxes still surrounded us, and I needed to find my little saucepan for a recipe I wanted to try.

Giving in to temptation, I unpacked the necessaries while storing the rest upstairs in our new handy-dandy loft which would one day be our craft area. The idea behind this decision was that if no one could see the mess from the main floor, we could store things up there. During the next three years, the loft became the repository for records (the vinyl kind), yarn, craft supplies, old clothes, Christmas decorations, small pieces of furniture, tools, empty boxes that we can't throw out (the computer came in that one!), and a ceiling fan purchased two years ago that still needs to be installed.

Every year on New Year's Eve, among the resolutions to eat healthier and exercise more, I resolve to organize our loft. I resolve that this is the year I will dig down through the sedimentary layer of magazines and yarn to the hard packed granite of packed boxes. I will create a usable craft room, storage area and a sweet little guest area for kids. Goodbye, old satellite dish! Time to unpack the photo boxes and albums. My passport will be unearthed. I start planning the layout of the bedroom area and dream of leaving my sewing machine out and creating my paper-cut collages on the dedicated crafting table.

This year, I made an additional resolution for all of my resolutions: baby steps. Each large project must contain small steps I could complete in an hour or less. This way I could convince myself to stand up and go complete something without having to devote my entire weekend to cleaning out the loft. I'm just too lazy otherwise....or maybe I just have too many things I'd rather do. (Rather being the most important word in that sentence.)

So as I stood there, contemplating and attempting to avoid the magazines sliding from the tops of their perilously high stacks while I dug through sacks of yarn, I generated a plan. A lovely "baby steps" plan.

First, the yarn. When we moved into the house, my sweet honey-bunny pulled a chest of drawers upstairs. She placed it by a window and stacked our wireless router on top. Consequently, I can surf the internet from almost anywhere in the house, which I love! Also, she left all of those lovely drawers empty and revealed to me just the other day that she had no plans for them.

Yep. Those drawers are mine now. By color and type, I will pack my yarn stash in them, nice and tidy. And in order to keep the clutter to a minimum, I will always check my stash before I buy more yarn.

Really I will.

Unless I need more of one type than I have. Or I have the wrong color. Or I have the right color and the wrong texture.

Which is the only reason that I placed that order today.

Once I've completed that task, I will toss my hoarded cooking magazines. Yes, I keep all my cooking magazines: Martha Stewart Living, Cook's Illustrated, Bon Appetit, Gourmet, Southern Living, Taste of Home, Cook's Country. Every month, a new batch arrives and every month I pour through the pages, picking recipes out that I want to try. Then, I stack them into a pile and plop them into my magazine rack. After a couple of months, I go through the stack again and take all the cooking magazines upstairs to the "research pile." My plan is that one day I will go through the "research pile" and copy all of the recipes I want to try into my computer's recipe database.

HAHAHAHAHAHAAH!

I will never take that stack of magazines and my computer and type the recipes into my database, nor will I try the recipes out once I've done all that work.

Why? Because six new recipe magazines just arrived!

Also, because when I have a prodigal pork tenderloin or set of chicken breasts, before I delve into my computerized recipe database for the answer, I will always go through my latest magazines, online recipe databases and cookbooks.

Don't get me wrong! I love my computerized recipe database and use it all the time, but mostly for recipes that I already know I like and want to use again. All new finds and old classics go into the recipe database. I just don't go there for ideas or to try new recipes.

Sometimes, I just have to face the facts.

So, *sigh* my magazine stack can go. Some of them will inevitably stay as a collection (Martha Stewart, Cook's Illustrated, Cook's Country), but the rest - out of here! I will ruthlessly and harshly recycle those stacks until they are gone. I will toss that Bon Appetit with that beautifully inaccessible cake on the cover as well as that Gourmet with that gorgeous roast!

I will.

After all, Lesbian Law #1: Never Underestimate the Power of the Lesbian Housewyfe.

I'll start right after I finish this television show. And try out that new sourdough bread recipe. And toss those poinsettias left over from Christmas.

Darn! Is it the New Year again already?

·♥·♥·♥·♥·♥·

THE CONDIMENT GANG

A couple of months after moving into our house, Stephanie and I bought a refrigerator. Stainless steel double doors with handy water and ice dispensers promised an organized display of beverages, vegetables, fruits and meats, all within my grasp. The wide shelves, the deep drawers, and the little box for eggs all promised a virtuous life filled with perfectly portioned meals and leftovers only at Thanksgiving. I even believed that I could fit a big fat turkey on the center shelf for those big banquets at the holidays.

As I stood in the middle of Sears, staring into the depths of our soon-to-be refrigerator, I forgot about the condiments.

Our refrigerator is empty only twice during our life in a house: once when we move in and again when we move out. In accordance with Lesbian Law #85: "Waste not, lest you be judged," we always transfer all of our food to our new house and that includes the giant laundry basket of condiments.

This is due to the influence of my mother-in-law, the "condiment woman." We have a friend who used to go over to her house when he was a teenager, open the door of the fridge and see empty shelves and a door full of condiments. I suspect he drank the ketchup, although that confession never appeared. He tried to get high on catnip once, so I wouldn't put anything past him.

Currently, out of the forty-nine items residing in my refrigerator door, six items moved to our latest home with us back in June of 2002. These are:

Thai Green Basil Curry Paste
Thai Red Curry Paste
Whole Grain Mustard (one of four different bottles of mustard)
Liquid Smoke
Tabasco ™
Worcestershire Sauce

The liquid smoke, Tabasco™ and worcestershire sauce actually all moved from my sister-in-law's refrigerator when she moved to Atlanta back in the spring of 1999. Yes, I have three condiments in my refrigerator that date from the last century. (See Lesbian Law #85, above.)

Fourteen of the forty-nine jars and bottles were purchased within the last three months. Unfortunately, I also have to admit that two are different brands of dijon mustard and I believe the harissa paste could easily join the above ranks in a few years. How often can you use harissa paste? Ground chiles in oil with a moroccan flair went very well with my Easter lamb, but I don't know what else to do. Oh wait.... I'm sure that the six recipe magazines that land in my mailbox each month will have some suggestions.

After all, it was one of their "bright idea" recipes that got me into this.

This is how I came to own twenty-nine - count 'em - twenty-nine condiments that we bought between the summer of 2004 and the spring of 2006. Condiments that have made a home in my refrigerator door. They all have a story behind them. I become entranced with some new recipe and end up with most of a jar of mango chutney because, "that's nasty."

At least the review was concise.

Steph wants me to reiterate that it wasn't the condiment's fault; the recipe was the thing that went horribly awry.

Several years ago, Stephanie began drinking martinis regularly so an assortment of olives (pimento-stuffed, almond-stuffed, sicilian spiced, greek black) and three jars of pickled tomatoes (all with different sizes of tomatoes) joined the gang. She switched over to club soda with lime juice last summer, so the leftover olives and tomatoes now languish in my refrigerator door.

Summer here in the Yampa Valley brings the opening of our farmer's markets. Sweet Pea, the perennial favorite, along with two weekend-only temporary setups, bring local and organic produce into our shopping radius. In the depths of summer, I trundle under the green corrugated plastic roof and dip into boxes of red tomatoes that smell like summer gardens in full bloom, ripe soft peaches that smell like golden cobbler doled out lavishly by my grandmother, and red potatoes that smell like...well, dirt, but they taste like butter. The plethora of fresh scents and sweet tastes dazzle my winter-starved senses and I end up with not only way too many fresh veggies and fruits, but also dipping sauces, salad dressings and jams.

I blame those on the heat.

The Liquid Smoke Gang (named after its oldest member) confronts me whenever I open the refrigerator, jeering and taunting. Their favorite chant is "You can't toss me! You might need me!" Then they scurry back to their places and giggle.

What they don't know is that every condiment can go bad (except maybe liquid smoke) or be used up (except maybe liquid smoke). I'm arming myself to do battle!

While during my monthly perusal of the refrigerator results in tossing the old leftovers and desiccated vegetables, I rarely touch the condiments in the door. All of that is changing this summer. This summer, I'm ruthlessly organizing my refrigerator - including the door!

First, I protect myself with rubber gloves. The next thing to go is my conscience which screams Lesbian Law #2: "Reduce, reuse, recycle." I refuse to open some of those jars, much less touch them with my bare hands. With the trash can conveniently settled near the refrigerator, the door opens.

The mango chutney goes first. I'll never make that recipe again. Next, I check out the jams, jellies and syrups. One of those suckers has something fuzzy on the top. The weird tapanade that no one ever liked - out of here! Ruthless desperation invades my body and I barely look before I drop each condiment into the trash.

After the carnage, I make a list of my most used condiments and make sure they are positioned correctly. Ketchup, barbeque sauce, mayonnaise, dijon mustard, butter, yeast (I know they aren't really condiments, but they are in the refrigerator door along with three bottles of wine and a container of ginger syrup), soy sauce, the four almost empty bottles of salad dressing that need to be consumed, worcestershire sauce (it's a huge bottle), Tabasco™ (I only use 1/8-1/4 teaspoon per recipe), and, finally, anchovy paste (used a single tea-spoon at a time whenever I make chicken Provençal). These aren't the only condiments in the door, but they are the most prominent and my refrigerator door now has space for another couple bottles of wine.

Just in time for summer!

Those condiments have learned their lesson.

Except, maybe, the liquid smoke.

"GET RID OF ALL THOSE OLIVES" MARTINI PARTY

Now that your house is full of different types of olives from the last three parties that you've thrown (since you bought a new bottle per party), time to throw a Martini Party!

Trés chic.

Trés bon.

Trés Lesbian Law #2: Reduce, reuse, recycle.

First off, make sure you have the right music. The entire Rat Pack (Frank, Dean, and Sammy) should make an appearance, and Diana Krall won't be out of place either. Pull out Ella and Billie, too. These swingers keep everyone bouncing while simultaneously keeping them feeling cool.

Now, glassware. I love the Deco cone with that long thin stem. Yep, you've got to use the martini glasses. Nothing else will fill the bill.

Cocktail picks are a must for stabbing those olives and getting them into your glasses. The job becomes so much easier because you can just let your guests pick the olive combination for their drinks. "Stabbing the Olive" – a great party game!

No, that game doesn't sound dirty, unless you're making dirty martinis!

Food should be easy to eat with the fingers and stationed about the room so that everyone can comfortably mingle and munch.

Now, since you already have olives, you are set to party! Simply set a time and date and invite your friends.

***

MY SWEET HONEY-BUNNY'S FAVORITE VODKA MARTINI

The barest bit of dry vermouth
    1-2 oz chilled vodka
olives or pickled tomatoes

Fill the bottom of the vermouth bottle cap with vermouth. Pour into your martini glass and swirl around, coating the glass. Drain the excess away. Pour vodka into the glass. Stab one to three olives or pickled tomatoes onto your handy dandy cocktail pick and gently drop it into the glass.

Serve with a smile, and perhaps the ubiquitous apron and pearls of June Cleaver.

·♥·♥·♥·♥·♥·

LIQUOR LA

M ost people, including myself, have a box of Christmas ornaments which bring a flood of nostalgia every year. Every
ornament plucked from the box is held lovingly for a moment.

"This iridescent glass ball is from our trip to Mount St. Helens. We
bought it in a restaurant on the Spirit Lake Memorial Highway on the
way back from seeing the volcano. Do you remember that day? It was
the anniversary of the blast in 1980. The ball is made from the ash."

"After Grammy passed away, Uncle Dave gave us this box of glass
ornaments. She used them every year until my cousin borrowed them
for his tree. After Christmas, he lost his mind and tossed the tree out
without taking any of the decorations or lights off. These were the ones
we saved."

"My mother gave me this little bead mouse she bought at a bazaar
in Mayflower, Arkansas. We always hung a little mouse similar to this
upside down by its tail on the bottom branches for the cats to beat
up."

I love Christmas.

However, I have another place that I like to go and remember the
special moments of my life. I call it "the liquor cabinet."

All of my liquor (except the wine and beer) sits on top of my
refrigerator. I know I read somewhere that you should never store your

liquor on top of the fridge, but I really have no other place in my sweet, cozy home. Plus, this positioning definitely keeps it out of the reach of most children and pets. Our two precious kittens barging full-tilt through the house have laid waste to a lot more than my scotch, but that's my fault. What's the point of having nice things if you never use them? I suppose they don't get broken that way. Precocious cats are a danger to fine china.

Each time I clamber up on my little stepladder to pull down my scotch for my weekly shot, I am assailed by memories of the past.

Steph went through a phase where her weekly cocktail was the vodka martini. (Let's keep the groans to a minimum. She had an unfortunate experience with gin as a teenager, and never recovered to embrace the classic gin martini.) We keep a bottle of vodka in the freezer and use only that for the martini. I fill the bottom of the cap of the vermouth bottle (extra-dry, please) with the vermouth and then pour it directly into the glass. A swirl around the entirety of the cone to coat the glass and then dump any remaining into the sink. Fill the glass with one to two ounces of vodka (depending on the harshness of the week) and then drop in one to three olives or pickled tomatoes speared onto a swizzle stick into the drink. Sit and sip. As I recall, after one of these, Steph just sits.

I felt so like June Cleaver fixing Ward his evening cocktail.

Grammy Loel (Steph's maternal grandmother) visited over Christmas and New Years for the turn of the millenium. (I say this for 1999-2000 just like most of the people in the world. I really don't care about the whole debate between this date and the one for 2000-2001. Chill out. It's all over already.)

Anyway, since Grammy was coming up for the holidays, we asked her if she'd like us to buy her something special to drink for the celebration. Therefore, a bottle of amaretto sits on the fridge, still mostly full.

In 1999, we spent a week in France travelling on the Canal-du-Midi. Our friend Lynda's fiftieth birthday celebration carried us over the Atlantic and dropped us on a lazy canal, complete with locks to navigate (just enough work to make you feel like you deserved that bottle of wine). On our way back to Paris (a trip which took another two weeks as we traveled to Barcelona and then up the west coast of France), we stopped at a small bed and breakfast outside Tourouve. The older couple who ran the place took pity on us and served us dinner as well as breakfast since there were no restaurants near the location, and I think they also sensed the weariness pervading our bodies.

This simple dinner is one of my favorite gastronomic experiences of all time. We started with sauteed mushrooms topped with a small square of puff pastry. The husband harvested the mushrooms from the hills that very day and Steph ooohed and aaaahed about the fresh earthy flavor. For the main course, a dish they called "swiss steak," which turned out to be a rosti, a classic dish much like a large potato pancake with ham and topped with a fried egg. As I dislike eggs, I picked around the middle and blamed my lack of appetite on a cold I had been fighting since we got to France.

Isn't that always the way it is? You go on vacation and suddenly come down with a cold or the flu or some nasty something! I assume that the reason this happens is because we go on vacation and let down, and then the little buggies come at us when we're weak. Anyway, back to the event.

The old man stared at me for a moment and then took off for the kitchen, re-emerging with an unlabeled bottle filled with an amber liquid. He filled shot glasses and plopped them down in front of each of us.

"This will cure you." He stated in French and the other fellow staying at the inn translated for the stupid American.

I stared at the glass and then figured that if there was anything deadly in it, the alcohol would have killed it.

I sipped and then slurped down that shot of homemade calvados with relish. Our hostess followed our digestif with a real tarte tatin, made with the same calvados from fresh apples plucked from the tree that day.

I definitely felt healthier.

So, a bottle of calvados from Charles de Gaulle airport sits atop my refrigerator along with two others I bought last year to compare. That trip also stored a bottle of cognac and one of poire william, a pear brandy that could be likened to some sort of fuel, in our "cabinet."

One yummy poire william drink is a pear champagne cocktail. Drop a tablespoon of poire william in the bottom of a champagne flute. Place a slice of pear into the glass and fill to the rim with sparkling wine. Don't drop the pear in after the wine or that yummy champagne explodes out of the top of the glass and fizzes all over your counter.

Sticky!

Sit down to drink because by the end, you can't feel your legs anymore.

Being the general recycle bin for most of our family, you will find bottles of grappa, Kahlua and vermouth which magically appeared in our collection when Jack, my mother-in-law's companion, moved to Asheville, North Carolina a few years ago.

We are pretty darn good hostesses, so there is a bottle of Kamora (a coffee liquer similar to Kahlua) we bought when our friend Emil visited, three bottles of port (each half-empty) which we received as hostess gifts and a bottle of gin we keep around only for our friend MB who drinks gin martinis.

In the realm of the unusual, we have two bottles of Godiva chocolate liqueur, a full bottle of Hypnotique, two bottles of sake and one bottle of a stone pine liqueur which tastes like a pine forest with a kick. Bottles of cassis, Remy Red, and (horror of horrors for my sweet honey-bunny) citron vodka are reminders of our first year in our current abode when I was in love with pink drinks. A cosmopolitan graced my hand once a week throughout the summer, followed by club soda and Remy Red through the fall and then kir royales (sparkling wine with a splash of cassis) for the holidays.

Just so you know, I prefer Zardetto Prosecco for my kir royales and Veuve Cliquot for my straight champagne drinking. In case you were wondering....

Each bottle holds a memory as sweet and dear to me as the liquor inside. And the best part is, when the liquor disappears, I use the bottles for homemade vinegar and syrups. (Lesbian Law #2: "Reduce, reuse, recycle.")

Unless they have a screw cap. There's no romance in a screw cap.

Don't forget Lesbian Law#1: "Never Underestimate the Power of a Lesbian Housewyfe."

I'm going to have a cocktail.

LA's Favorite Cosmopolitan

I lost my taste for vodka in the fall semester of my freshman year of college when I got drunk for the first time. Vodka and lemonade, vodka and Coke and I think maybe some vodka and Dr. Pepper. I actually don't remember that part, but people told me that this particular concoction appealed quite a bit to me. On that same night, Dukakis lost the presidential election to George Bush. I remember this part because for the following four years, people I didn't know would come up to me and say "Dukakis lost!" Apparently, I was a bit upset about it.

Now that many years have passed, I've discovered that an icy concoction which doesn't reveal the taste of straight vodka can now be imbibed. I first tried this drink when I was out "drinking with the girls."

1/4 cup Cranberry juice
1 oz. Citrus vodka
1/2 oz. Rose's lime juice
1/2 oz. Triple Sec

Pour all ingredients into a shaker over ice. Shake, shake, shake and strain into the beautiful deco cone of a martini glass. Sip, smile and look classy.

·❤·❤·❤·❤·❤·

BETTER BUTTER

Last night I got home from my writer's group and found my sweet honey-bunny standing over the sink sorting and washing plums.

"You are so lucky I decided to do this," she exclaimed as I entered the house. "These plums were a gross moldy fermenting mess."

The kitchen trash can had been pulled from beneath the sink and filled with rotted nasty plums.

"We were making plum wine!" She asserted.

All of this plum nonsense started last weekend when our cousin Laurie called.

"My brother-in-law picked a whole bunch of plums from his tree and brought them up. They are the black-skinned with yellow inside kind. Do you want them? I'm not going to have time to make jelly."

A moment of trepidation later, I spoke. "Sure."

"I'll just drop them off on your porch."

"We'll be here."

"Just in case. You know. You might leave. I'll leave them on the porch."

"Okay, then. Thanks."

I expected a plastic grocery bag full of plums. A box of pectin got added to the grocery list and my jar supply looked sufficient.

Several hours later, I discovered a large kitchen garbage bag full of plums on my porch. No wonder she wanted to drop and run! That sneaky gal!

With varying degrees of ripeness, so I knew I was in plum trouble. However, instead of doing the right thing and digging in immediately, I just pulled the bag inside the door so the bears wouldn't get to the plums.

Just imagine! A yard full of bits of plastic and plum pit shit!

Maybe that would have been a better answer for my conundrum.

Anyway, I pulled the bag inside and went back to watching tennis.

Okay, so realistically, I could have washed and sliced plums and watched the women's final of the US Open, but then, when would my knitting have gotten finished?

One obsession at a time please!

So the plums languished in a closed garbage bag by the front door.

On Tuesday morning, I opened the bag so the plums could get some air and not completely rot away.

On Tuesday evening, my sweet honey-bunny closed the bag to keep the smell of rotting plums contained.

On Wednesday, I found a recipe for plum butter. Spices were necessary to cover up the varying tastes.

And then I let them sit until Thursday.

Which brings me back to my sweet honey-bunny, standing over the sink, sorting plums with tongs because they were so gross she didn't even want to touch them.

Of course, I saw all of this as evidence of my sloth as a housewife and immediately began helping.

"As soon as I'm done washing these, I'm going to chop them up so you can do that first step."

The plum butter recipe started with heating the sliced plums and a little sugar. Since I'm way too short to reach the stockpot I store at the very the top of the pot rack, my stepstool made an appearance so I could pull it down. With the interior spotless, I left the pot within easy reach of my sweet honey-bunny.

Time to make dinner!

While I assembled the salad, my industrious sweetie toiled away until she couldn't stand up any longer. I fixed her some toast as an appetizer and sent her into the den to control the television and keep me entertained.

While the steaks grilled and more bread toasted, I finished pitting and quartering the fruit.

After a filling dinner of steak, salad and toast, I threw the dishes into the dishwasher, filled the sink with sudsy water, tossed some sugar into the plums and set them on a low heat to slowly warm and macerate. While combining the sugar and fruit, I amazed at the fact that this mass of black, yellow and white would become a single deep magenta.

Jellies, jams, butters and preserves really show off the true kitchen chemistry. Fruit changes and evolves and becomes a sweet spread perfect for toast or cake filling or a tart. Little miracles of science in my own home!

Anyway, the plums did their thing while I finished washing the salad bowl and assorted knives and generally got the kitchen back in working order. Then, I took a bit of time to actually read the recipe.

Yeah. I'm always a little behind the ball that way.

My plan had been to complete the recipe through the second step of pureeing the hot mixture. Then, instead of cooking that mixture down in the pot for several hours, I would let my slow cooker do the work overnight.

Well, when I read the recipe, I found this: "Add the sugar and spices, bring to a boil and then reduce heat while still maintaining an active simmer. Cook five-ten minutes, or until mixture sheets off the spoon."

Since the clock only read 8:30, I could complete the entire recipe and be in bed by 10! I opened a new package of jars and dug through my cabinets for extras. With these two endeavors, 14 jars, 12-8 ounce and 2-12 ounce became available. I quickly washed them and set the sealing lids in hot water.

Ready for canning!

The food processor pureed my hot fruit coarsely. Kitchen magic transformed the mixture from slightly pink-tinged green chunks to a deep hot pink flecked with dark purple. I transferred each batch (after batch after batch) into a bowl and then dumped the whole thing back into the pot. The pureeing process left the food processor, counter, stove and my shirt spotted with dark pink sticky blotches.

Yum!

My puree was still a bit tart, so more sugar joined the amalgamation along with cinnamon, nutmeg, cloves and allspice. Now time to bring the whole thing to a boil, stirring occasionally while I washed my sticky implements.

When the spicy puree finally bubbled, I reduced the heat and cooked it, stirring constantly, until it reached a soft, coherent consistency. At that point, the lava-like substance was an almost brown magenta. I quickly jarred and sealed the butter, and set it upside-down on a towel for inversion canning. After only 12 of the jars had been filled, my mission was almost complete. I set the timer for five minutes and dumped the pot, spoon, and ladle into the still warm dishwater. As I finished the washing, the timer beeped.

I turned the jars upright and headed off to bed, feeling pretty darn righteous. There's nothing like the success of an unexpected chore to make you feel like an upstanding member of society.

With canning, however, there's still one more step – one that you can't do anything about. If you can using the inversion method, the jars complete their seal over the next 24 hours. Their little tops sink down with a pop, sealing in all that yummy goodness. But you don't know if the seal has been successful until the first jar pops, so there's always that moment of uncertainty.

But, just as I slipped between the sheets at 9:59PM, I heard the first seal snap in the kitchen. I turned off the light and slipped into sleep, listening to the jars pop in the darkness.

I don't know why I don't trust myself. After all, Lesbian Law #1 is Never Underestimate the Power of a Lesbian Housewyfe.

Now for the crabapples my sister-in-law dropped off yesterday.

PLUM BUTTER FOR BUSY DAYS

Shortcuts are okay.
    They are legal.
    They are practical.
    They are necessary.
    And sometimes, they yield delicious fruit butter.

    1.5lb plums, pitted
    1.5 cups sugar, divided
    1/2 teaspoon cinnamon
    1/8 teaspoon nutmeg
    1/8 teaspoon ground cloves
    1/8 teaspoon allspice

Process plums in a food processor to puree. Put in slow cooker and add 1/2 cup sugar. Turn on high and cook for three hours. Add remaining sugar and spices. Partially cover and maintain heat for one to three hours. Test for doneness by pouring a spoonful onto a chilled plate. If no rim of liquid forms around the edge of the butter, it is done. Put into jars and seal.

·♥·♥·♥·♥·♥·

THE PARTY GUIDE

R ecently, the lovely Lesbian Housewyfe faced a common situation: my wonderful wyfe came home and, as she walked
through the door, said, "How about we give a party?"

I considered a moment, realizing that this could transform two days
of my quiet life into total chaos in exchange for a few moments of
enjoyment between cleaning up spilled drinks and washing these same
glasses quickly so someone else could spill a new fruity iced alcoholic
beverage onto my barely recognizable (and so recently mopped) floor
before confronting a mountain of dishes and an entirely new sticky
mess all over my house the morning after. With trepidation, I forced
the word "Okay" through my lips and closed my eyes. After all, only
two things could happen next. The first, and the one devoutly hoped
for, is that we were going to discuss the idea over a nice dinner and start
the preparations the next day. The second option was that my sweet
considerate compassionate wyfe would say, "GREAT!", open the door
again, and several people would file into the house behind her uttering
the three little words no unprepared hostess ever wants to hear:

"Where's the beer?"

I was lucky.

I was stocked.

Even if I hadn't been, I don't see the run for beer as a hassle in this situation. When I escape to restock the ol' liquor cabinet, along with whatever party fixin's I deem necessary (like chips, salsa, and a fifth of scotch for the surprised hostess), I take a little extra time to pull myself together and think up some good excuses for the fact that I didn't dust that afternoon. Yes, I know I was watching the PBS gardening marathon all afternoon, but I wanted to sound more productive than that. The added plus is that by the time I think up something plausible, almost everyone is gone.

Sometimes it happens.

Anyway, if I can't seem to escape this phenomenon by avoidance, I find that guilt can be a major tool in getting help cleaning up. Don't laugh. You know that all us housewives get to clean everything up. It's just a fact of life. When it comes to party cleanup, everyone seems to lose their handbook of Lesbian Laws, no matter what Lesbian Law #20 says (Household duties are to be divided equally among all members of the residence unless heavy lifting is involved in which case this particular job falls under the domain of the butchy babe.). Maybe we should attach an amendment like Lesbian Law #42a: One must always assist one's partner in any special or unexpected chores such as party clean-up or strange sheet stains, etc.

Hey, that's kinda poetic, huh?

If, however, the party is not an ambush and I have time to prepare and plan the event, there are several questions I answer before I begin to buy the party favors. The first is "What kind of party do we want?" I have divided the concept of "Party" into three different categories, as I am wont to do.

A) DDT

These "Drinking and Dancing Topless" parties are those clear the brain, drown your sorrows, lose your inhibitions, and dance 'til dawn parties that you used to go to and perhaps even hold in your small dorm room in college. Now, of course, you can only take the experience once every two or three years. Your next one is probably scheduled for some time around the turn of the millennium. While not everyone chooses to disrobe at these parties, we all know that one woman who just can't seem to keep her shirt on once she's had a couple of wine coolers - and it's always wine coolers, isn't it. DDT's are the most poisonous parties of all. Especially if the legs on your kitchen table aren't reinforced. No one should be faced with the sight of a half naked, hung over woman struggling to stand in the debris of one's furniture first thing in the morning. It's not a pretty sight. Trust me.

B) ET

Eating and Talking parties (a.k.a. dinner parties) I have known range from the simplicity of a casual brunch to the formality of a gourmet Thanksgiving dinner. These parties are the most difficult to prepare because of the sheer amount of work that goes into making a meal but the payoff of a comfortable atmosphere and great conversation make the effort more than worth it. One of the best parts about ET's is that, at the end, everyone usually goes home. One last note: although flexible in form, dinner parties are difficult to expand in terms of guest list. RSVP was created for these parties. Always use it.

C) BRA

Otherwise known as "Bribe, Reward, Acknowledgement" parties, these form themselves around big events like a friend's move, a movie premier, or making it to Friday without quitting your job. Sometimes you buy the beer and sometimes your boss does. Your main role in these settings is to sit back, drink the beverage of your choice, and dish the dirt for a couple of hours. These mostly impromptu and casual parties are the biggest culprits of sluggish mornings and can quickly mutate into either of the other forms of party. Most of the time, these are the ones that will surprise you at the door after a day at home alone.

These parties can be the most impressive parties you attend, also. I went to one party recently which definitely fit into this BRA. Oh yes, they do let me out of my little house sometimes and I manage not to disappoint.

You see, through connections which seem tenuous at best, my sweet love and I attended a screening of the new film adaptation of Richard III starring Sir Ian McKellan who was also in attendance. Then, the three of us (well, actually the fifty of us) rushed to an excellent and completely expensive restaurant downtown for a lovely reception with lots of free wine and food.

And I got to meet Sir Ian McKellan.

And talk to him.

And he was totally gracious and wonderful and not at all like Richard which, truthfully, was exactly what I expected.

My extra bonus was that Stephanie and I got to him at just the right time so that he was tipsy enough to be talkative.

Here is how it went:

I joined the group of people surrounding Sir Ian at a point when the crowd was mainly composed of people I knew. I tried to look cool and discuss certain points of interest with my sweet honey bunny but it is really hard to do that when you're just a starstruck staring idiot. Anyway, that approach seemed to work because, before long, he spoke to me. "I don't think I've been introduced to you yet." So I introduced myself as LA Bourgeois and he said, and I quote directly, "Bla?" When we finally got that name thing corrected, someone distracted him and he felt the need to depart. He shook Steph's hand and she said, "It's been lovely talking to you, Sir Ian."

His response was, "Well, we haven't talked at all." and he stayed and we discussed the movie and laughed and had a good time until our friend Michael (our entree to this soiree) came and stole him away from us poor lesbians. Goddamn queens get 'em every time. So we stole him back. But just to say farewell and let him get back to his wine and photographers. All in all, I think I did okay for my first meeting with a famous person. He laughed at my jokes and enjoyed my company for the time it was foisted upon him.

But that wasn't all...

1) My friend, Dr. X, who I don't want to alienate, told her "I met a famous person once" story the day we all went to the movie. Apparently, she and some of her friends were in New York one day and they saw the crowd exiting the theatre where Patrick Stewart was performing his one man Christmas Carol. They decided to hang out at the stage door and see him. Well, while they were waiting, Dr. X (then Graduate Student X) admonished all of her friends to be very cool when they met Patrick. So, as soon as he exited the theatre and walked near her, she screamed, "I love you, Patrick."

When asked about his reaction, she said he took two steps to the left and searched desperately for an escape route.

Determined not to repeat this performance, Dr. X was very cool at the reception until she discovered that she was talking to one of the men who was starring in the touring production of "Dial M for Murder" as if he were Sir Ian McKellan.

Oops.

My friend, queen of the goobers.

It's strange how, after a party, all the "party tales" make you sound like you've just attended a real life soap opera, isn't it? Oh well, on to the rest of my stories.

2) One of Stephie's friends that I don't know very well was talking to Terry, Michael's cute husbynd. Knowing what a thrill it can be to meet a famous person, he leaned over and graciously asked her if she wanted him to introduce her to Sir Ian.

Stephie's friend, who did attend the screening, immediately answered, "Who's Sirian?"

Our only response was "You know, that new model from Africa."

3) I met this guy and his girlfriend who were touring with the "Dial M for Murder" production starring Roddy McDowell (not to drop names or anything so crass as that. Who the hell am I kidding? If I could run through all the streets of Denver yelling "I met Roddy McDowell and Sir Ian McKellen" and still feel cool about it, I would.) and I could swear that I have seen him on PBS or maybe A&E on one of their mysteries. We met them in kind of a weird way and basically they attacked us because they overheard that we lived here and wanted to know where the best skiing was. Stephie told them and we went on our way.

The strange part of this story is that he was the only one out of the cast besides Roddy McDowell (How the hell did all these Brits converge at once upon a western city such as Denver?) that I recognized. The lead female was being played by some woman from Robocop and the lead male by some guy from Dynasty. I had to admit that, even though I know quite a bit about popular culture, there are some areas where I'm rather insulated.

Thank God.

4) Roddy McDowell shoved me while he was trying to get to Sir Ian to bid him adieu.

5) The movie was really really good.

Well, I think I've fawned enough. Back to the real subject.

After deciding which kind of party I want to enjoy, the guest list becomes the most important thing in my life. The people you invite to your party form the atmosphere. Several types of party guests are in existence today. Since the genus contains many different species, I will only list the most prolific. Lots of the party participants are just variations on one of these general themes anyway.

The Party Girl/Boy Toy - Basically harmless, undresses at the slightest tip of a glass then tends to break it. Frequently clueless, she has been overheard as saying things such as "Who's Sirian?" Unrepentant flirt, usually ends up in the bathroom having sex.

Intellectual - talky person who brings evocative ideas into the conversation, generally an academic. Can be an overenthusiastic boor if trying to be cool. May also be known as "Queen of the Goobers."

Queen Bee - seen only at the most important events, tends to upend everything to check out the marking. For concrete reference, see all references to Roddy McDowell above.

Clown - the life of the party. Groups cluster around this person. No conversation but great entertainment.

Cuckold - sworn enemy of the Party Girl/Boy Toy. His/Her life partner (although perhaps not for long) is the one in the bathroom. Dangerous to combine the two types in one room after this occurrence.

Great Friends - These are the people who gather with you in a small corner of the party and just comfortably make great conversation like, say, Sir Ian McKellen (just to drop names, if I may. What's the use of going to all these parties if you're not going to use the experience shamelessly afterwards?).

Hostess - Would any party be complete without her? She can be seen everywhere, wearing a harried smile and carrying at least two more things than she should.

A balanced mixture of these types is a good combination for any party, but keep in mind the pitfalls inherent in every situation. If you aren't careful, when you give in and invite that one party girl you know, you may have changed your lovely dinner party into a wild evening of raucous sex and loud music. More than one of your grandmother's crystal glasses will be sacrificed on the alter of her libido. The same goes for that quiet and intelligent woman who provides the most provocative conversation at your dinner party. She may be the most interesting person sitting down, but totally out of place at your huge blow-out. Truly, it is easier for her to make the transition than your alcoholic party girl, but it's important that she doesn't just end up in a bare little corner with you baby-sitting her all night. I realize that Lesbian Law #20 says "When giving a party, one must invite everyone one knows, since leaving someone out would be rude and potentially dangerous to the other person's self esteem" but remember, you have things to do!

The last question I must ask myself is, "Do we have enough plates?" Now it is time for the real nitty gritty. This question can limit your guest list or expand your china cabinet. Careful consideration of your abilities and resources will provide a basic skeleton for quite a party. Everything is based upon a foundation and this is yours for a party. "No one will rave if you don't have enough chairs or glasses." Thank you, Etiquette Annie!

Where did she come from?

Anyway, everyone likes to come to a party where the hostess is prepared. My basic foundation of party needs are usually covered by an empty trash can (or cans, depending on whether or not I want to do dishes afterwards), proper dishes and glasses (whether plain paper or fine crystal is your decision), enough chairs for comfort, and a great music selection.

And don't forget, I know what I'm doing. After all, Lesbian Law #1 is "Never Underestimate the Power of a Lesbian Housewyfe."

I give good party.

More than most of the time.

QUICK PARTY PROVISIONS

Creating a party with the stuff on hand can be challenging, especially if you are about to head out to the store when the party arrives. However, a close inspection of the cabinets and freezer can reveal your hidden ingenuity. I keep several things on hand just in case.

Always on the lookout for sales, I stock up on frozen appetizers as space allows. That way I can pull out a box, toss the little frozen bits into the oven and emerge with a smorgasbord of tasty warm goodness from which my guests can choose as they sip their wine, beer or cocktail of the moment.

I also like sweets such as ice cream bars and popsicles for those hot summer days, and those keep indefinitely. Along with that, watermelon granita can serve as a classy dessert or a quick drink addition in a pinch. Once, an unexpected guest got served watermelon mojitos since we were out of tequila. Minty rummy icy goodness right there. Yeah baby.

A quick scan of my refrigerator will always reveal tasty salsa, a sack of carrot sticks, an assortment of cheeses and tons of condiments to be spread on whatever bread or crackers are around. The same amount of time in my pantry uncovers tortilla chips, several different types of crackers, some sort of nuts and more unopened condiments.

Appropriate trays, bowls and cutting boards emerge from the cupboards and serving silverware from the drawers. I keep a small package of paper napkins on hand for guests fingers. I quickly arrange the kitchen counter with my sweet honey-bunny's help, assuming that she's hooked everyone up with their drinks and set up the appropriate musical accompaniment.

Usually, we also have fresh seasonal fruit available on that counter

– apples or pears to be cut into wedges to go with brie, berries, plums, peaches, mangos, bananas, lemons and limes. Whatever is available at the farmer's market or produce aisle at any given time will find its way into my quick fix buffet.

I limit myself to thirty minutes for getting the food on the counter and then I sit down with my drink and enjoy my unexpected guests. Frankly, they are adults and can usually be safely trusted to cut their own cheese and fruit.

Watermelon mojito, anyone?

WATERMELON MOJITOS

During the summer, I always have watermelon sitting around, and since we stock more rum than tequila, I thought up this drink one hot day when I was craving a margarita.

1 oz. Rum
The juice of half a lime
A few mint leaves (like three to five per drink)
1/4 cup pureed watermelon
Ice
Club Soda

Crush your mint leaves and plop them into a tall glass along with lime juice, watermelon, and rum. Stir thoroughly to combine. Add ice (if necessary) and club soda to fill the glass. Give the drink another couple of stirs to make sure all the ingredients are distributed evenly through the glass.

Sit and sip.

·♥·♥·♥·♥·♥·

STRING THEORY

On a dark and stormy afternoon, I closed my eyes, braced myself and sprinted from my car across the parking lot to the post office. My mission: retrieve the mail.

Neither rain nor snow nor hail nor sleet nor.... Where's a postman when you need one?

My shirt stuck to me by the time I reached the doorway. Water filled the bottom of one of my shoes from an inadvertent splash into a deep puddle.

Opening a post office mailbox might be one of the most exciting things ever. You never know what could tumble out: a message from your mother, a bill, the latest Crochet magazine. Good news or bad, you've played your own little lottery and didn't lose a dollar in the process!

Today, a bomb was in my mailbox. A ticking time bomb reposing in a thick cream-colored envelope with a deckled edge and my name and address written in calligraphy.

I carefully pulled the wedding invitation from the box and studied the return address. My friend, Miss Petite Blondie Blue-Eyes, was getting married.

Each wedding invitation arrives and sets off a series of decisions and events culminating with the choice of the wedding gift. You don't want to spend too much (lest you are out more dollars than you can afford) or too little (lest they think you are a cheapskate). Sometimes they enclose information about a bridal registry at a local or online shop. Without that information, clues can be deduced from the wedding and reception location. Attending a potluck at the park, you can spend way less money on the gift than if you are having dinner at the chi-chi country club.

One way or the other, the gift must be perfect. You don't want to be the one who gave "that gift." The gift that sits on the top shelf in their garage or that they "accidentally" broke in their last move. Heaven forbid, your gift becomes the "white elephant" joke, circulated among friends for years before coming back to you with a funny card.

My solution has been a crocheted afghan. With the amount of time spent along with an appropriate yarn choice, the afghan truly suits any wedding from the local park to the swanky downtown hotel. Handmade by me, the gift of my time and their snuggling combines for an appropriate display of affection.

And even if they hate it, at least it's useful.

Now, however, I had to focus on the nuptials at hand. I stared at the invitation that evening, getting an idea of how my friend viewed her wedding and how that meshed with my view of her. A cream-colored thick envelope with a deckled edge and calligraphy means this person wants their wedding elegant and traditional, but opening the envelope revealed an independent soul who custom designed an eclectic invitation with a feather lovingly tucked into the fold. Elegant yet fun.

I can do that.

My "Wedding Ring" afghan consists of only two design guidelines: filet crochet and two interlocking rings in the middle. I'm basically lazy, so the filet crochet allows me to work the afghan up quickly while symbology of the interlocking rings is self-evident. Other than that, my imagination runs free and inserts anything that screams love, love, love into that pattern.

My perfect wedding ring afghan is five feet by eight feet to fit a queen sized bed or easily cover two people nestling on the couch. This rarely happens due to the fact that I always underestimate the amount of yarn necessary and because I have an alarming attachment to symmetry. If the afghan will be more symmetric in a smaller size, that's what you're stuck with.

Next, I choose the yarn. Fiber choice can make or break a snuggling experience. Now, if the couple is young, still moving from house to house or with a small child, my choice is consistently one hundred percent acrylic. Safe to wash and dry for the baby's barf and resilient enough to survive inevitable drops during moving, acrylic yarn creates a basically indestructible afghan that can live on the top of the couch for a long, long time. Luckily, the new fiber technologies mean that more and more acrylic colors, shapes and feels are available. My current favorite wedding yarn is hefty chenille in white, cream or champagne. Though, if I know the couple well, I may pick a brilliant red or wine color. Ah, the romance!

If the couple is older, on their second marriage or seemingly past the need for children, I find myself searching for more exotic fibers. Cotton, mohair and silk call to me from the shelves of my local yarn shop. Still, I migrate to soft, plushy fibers yearning for cuddling.

Miss Petite Blondie Blue-Eyes calls for bulky champagne chenille with a frame of eyelash yarn in the same color so she'll have a sophisticated plumpy afghan with a fuzzy border to tickle her nose.

Finally, I fulfill my mission. Luckily, I like to have something to do while I watch television and, luckily, I watch a lot of television. I try to schedule my afghans in the winter or around sporting events like tennis tournaments or the Olympics. However, if that scheduling fails, I simply station myself on the sofa with my bag of yarn, crochet hook, and a good mystery movie.

Nothing can stop the obsession to finish once I've truly gotten started on an afghan with a deadline. Late into the evening, find me crocheting in bed. Hot summer weather means hanging the afghan off the sofa so its warmth doesn't cook my legs. On wintry Rocky Mountain below-zero evenings, I huddle under a just-finished afghan while starting a new one.

Once, I was so late finishing the afghan that I crocheted in the car, finally finishing the thing in the hotel the night before the wedding. We stopped at a hobby shop on our way to the ceremony purchased cloth and ribbon to fashion a giant bag. There's nothing like the thrill of the gift as the wind whips through your car while your sweet honey-bunny runs back into the store to buy a pen to sign the card.

Who knew that it would be hard to fit a five by eight foot afghan into a three by six foot piece of cloth?

Whoops! We're usually so prepared!

Luckily, Miss Petite Blondie Blue-Eyes' afghan worked up quickly and turned into a five-by-five masterpiece of interlocking rings and hearts. I lovingly wrapped it (in my own house, even!) before inserting it with a lovely card into a box and returning to the post office on a beautiful sunny blue day to send it off to its new home.

Despite the trials and tribulations and long stretches of boring filet, I attempt to create every stitch with the love I have for my friend. She knows Lesbian Law#1: "Never underestimate the power of a Lesbian Housewyfe."

Nine months to finish the baby afghan!

·♥·♥·♥·♥·♥·

GIFT OF THE MAGI

Christmas, for the lovely Lesbian Housewyfe, seems to be a tur-
bulent time. For instance, as a people, Americans spend the
time leading up to that day of good cheer diving into shopping malls
and factory outlet stores, desperately searching for the perfect gift for
everyone on their little Christmas lists. We torture children all year
round with the idea that, if they aren't good girls and boys, they won't
be on the big granddaddy of all lists: Santa's. Our whole December is
aimed towards that single hour (or half-hour even) Christmas morning when we revel in the glory which is the gifting time.

As a role model for those American people, the Lesbian Housewyfe is duty bound to commit to this particular, or perhaps I should
say peculiar, American tradition. I mean, even with full knowledge
of Lesbian Law #8: "Take full responsibility for creating your own
traditions," I do tend to follow the crowd and attempt to embrace
cultural oddities if only for the experience.

However, I should note here that I am one of those horrible people
who always handmakes my gifts. The majority of my December (and
November, October, and part of September) is spent working my
little fingers to the bone, crocheting or cross-stitching or sewing some
little odd lot of stuff. The surprise also holds value for me so I usually
work on two or three projects at once so I can switch them out when

the current giftee is in the room. For example, one year I convinced Stephie to visit her sister in Steamboat Springs so I could finish my mother-in-law's (who lives with us) afghan. I mean really. Who on earth would put up with this sort of thing?

And yet, this year, I succumbed completely. My goal this Christmas was to buy my love the most special Christmas present she has ever received. Or, at least, whatever she wanted.

Steph is a wonderful handyperson, technical director, lighting and sound designer, and broken tile mosaic artiste extraordinaire. Therefore, I turned to the handyperson's mecca, the Sears Hardware Section.

Through careful listening, I managed to put together my specific instructions. I needed to procure a 12 volt Makita cordless drill with a keyless chuck, battery charger, and extra reserve battery. Yet, as the fateful day approached, I still desperately searched for an opportunity to unobtrusively travel to Sears and obtain the object of Steph's desire. My chance came when Barb, my mother-in-law, expressed a need to visit the hallowed halls and take advantage of a two hour sale. She wanted presents for the grandchildren and unknowingly assisted me.

I had my instructions. I had my ride. I had a really good diversion. The Christmas season had me in its grip.

I left Steph with Barb and the excuse that I needed some jeans. That was when the music started. I became acutely aware that I should have a holly jolly Christmas and that red-nosed reindeer, individually embraced as the harbingers of joy and light, should be shunned as a group. Reciting to myself, "Happiness equals shopping," I walked with purpose past the women's clothing to the escalator. A quick trip down and I was propelled into the vast hardware aisles. I could tell I was luckier than the rest as my eyes were not yet glazed over. The drill revealed itself and I nabbed it with all the fervor of a holiday shopper in the midst of a great sale. It was the only one left. I was just lucky no one else was around at the time. I couldn't handle a struggle at that point. I had been weakened by the flashing lights.

Trembling with excitement at finding my prize, I proceeded with purpose to the register where I waited impatiently for my turn to purchase, my virgin Sears credit card clenched in my warm fist. My time came shortly and I presented both card and drill to the clerk. He took one look at the tool I was thrusting towards him and said, "Now, are you sure you need such a powerful drill?"

I nodded mutely. Is he going to take away my drill? It's the perfect present! If I get Stephie this, she will love me forever. He can't have my drill. How will I have a holly jolly Christmas?!

I held out my credit card. He ignored it.

"What does your husband do?" He asked.

The spell was broken. It takes so little to break out of this particular phenomenon. Suddenly, I no longer cared if I had a happy Christmas. My early feminist training kicked in with a vengeance. I fell back on my newfound list of Lesbian Laws, searched through, and came up with the stinger. Lesbian Law #19: "Respond calmly under the duress of faulty logic and then make that fool suffer like no fool's ever suffered before."

I replied, "She's the technical director at a theater."

I wish I had taken my camera to the store. Never before have I seen so many conflicting emotions cross someone's face. A contemporary pictorial record of all the classic musical theater expressions wasted itself on my eyes only.

Do you know how much that could be worth? This was definitely a rare moment.

He ended the show by ringing me through with record speed and sending me gladly on my way. I admit I am a bit proud when I say that

I was, probably, his most discussed customer of the day.

Plus, I got a great price on a power drill! Small grocery store sales have nothing on those special holiday purchases found at a truly great discount. I love Sears.

I twittered my way back through the store and hid my gift in the back seat of a friend's car for deposit at our little home while Steph and I were visiting her sister.

Unbeknownst to me at the time, Steph had her own plans involving Sears. She managed to surprise me Christmas morning with a brand new Kenmore sewing machine. One day after we arrived back from Steamboat, she sneaked it inside, right under my nose! And, we purchased our gifts at the same time, transporting them back in the same car.

I am clueless sometimes, but isn't that part of my charm?

Maybe she's just really sneaky.

As the Christmas programming slowly wore off after the gift giving, I woke up enough to hear Barb say, "You girls are so stereotypical. Steph gets a drill and LA, a sewing machine. I thought you were more enlightened."

Whoops! Score one for the ingrained training of our civilization

After all, I am the Lesbian Housewyfe, and we are all familiar with Lesbian Law #1: "Never underestimate the power of the Lesbian Housewyfe."

Oh well. Have a Holly Jolly Christmas.

·♥·♥·♥·♥·♥·

THE HOLIDAY BLIZZARD

Menu-planning..... The thought sends me into a daydream of wandering through our local gourmet shop and picking up romantic items like caramelized shallot and fig spread so a magical osmosis will occur and I'll know what to do with it. Any excuse to pull out my cookbooks and this month's issues of my cooking magazines, dream about the pictures, and even go so far as to begin listing the ingredients for that obscure exotic supper builds a small bubble of joy.

Then, I look at my sweet honey-bunny sitting innocently in her chair and realize that all I need to serve each evening is a salad with some sort of protein alongside, and she will be perfectly content. I amend my plans (most of the time) and merge the exotic with the mundane.

My local grocery story doesn't carry lemongrass anyway.

By spending time creating menus and making grocery lists, I will get the correct supplies and use leftovers efficiently. With only the two of us and my plethora of available recipes, a lack of careful planning may mean a refrigerator full of food we'll never eat. And that's just wasteful, directly contradicting Lesbian Law #85:

"Waste not, lest you be judged."

Which is, of course, just common sense when you think about it.

The holidays, however, manage to release my inner Housewyfe

monster. No excuse exempts me from an orgy of menu planning, cooking exotic and untested recipes, and filling our refrigerator and pantry to overflowing. When else can you be drinking an entire bottle of a most luscious red wine and still profess to be working? Preparation and planning are at least as much fun as the actual meal.

The Housewyfe Monster creates menus featuring a seven pound spiral sliced ham (never an easy meal for two) or a beautifully elegant frenched rack of lamb. Exotic cheeses and salamis enter our refrigerator along with sheets of puff pastry and new condiments for dipping and spreading. The holidays lend their excuse to add to my collection of wine and liqueurs. Chambord, six bottles of claret and a bottle of Marsala work their magic and land in my liquor cabinet.

This year, menu-planning got an extra boost from the imminent arrival of the nieces. The elder of the two spent her fall semester in Ireland this year and called ahead to ensure plenty of good old American home cooking during the Christmas visit.

I would not disappoint.

First, a recipe in my Cook's Country magazine professed to create a perfect simulcrum of a popular frozen lasagna and could be stored for up to three months. With that recipe and the knowledge that we liked that particular lasagna on the odd occasion, I plucked the package of no-boil lasagna noodles which had been sitting sadly in the back of my pantry for several months and put together a shopping list.

Next, I realized that since we didn't know when or how long either of them would actually visit our home, a lentil soup served with perfection. Easy to heat-up quickly and hearty enough to fill after a full day of skiing or snowshoeing or whatever it is that these girls will do over this vacation with their mother or friends, this simple supper saves me from excessive work during the holiday season. Dinner number two!

For Christmas Eve, I found a recipe for a huge venison shepherd's pie from Nigella Lawson. I planned to halve the recipe and knew I would still have enough for eight!

Okay, can we just talk about Nigella Lawson for a moment? Scrumptious curves. Scrumptious cooking. Rawr.

That said, I can return to my actual topic.

Rawr.

A little flashback never hurt anyone.

A Christmas Day open house buffet needed a ham, rolls and all those fun cheeses and spreads to make it complete. I planned a cider, brown sugar and mustard glaze and surveyed the contents of the refrigerator for all those fun condiments. Healthy temptation added a platter of fresh carrots, sugar snap peas and red pepper slices with a ranch dressing dip. The girls were going out with their mother for dinner that evening, so I planned a simple but elegant (and completely mysterious) dinner for just myself and my sweet honey-bunny. Even when I left for the store, I was still unsure as to what I would serve there.

Breakfast one day would be the younger sister's favorite: Auntie Steph's famous pancakes. My sweet honey-bunny planned to make her little puffy ebleskivvers (a round-ball-like Swedish pancake served with butter and lingonberry jelly. Puffy little clouds of heaven).

Cake, cookies, candy and pie still haunted me. Cookbooks, magazines, and websites turned over in my search for the perfect sour cream pound cake. Lemon-crabapple thumbprints and chocolate coconut snowdrops would make up the cookie contingent. Enstrom's Toffee and a couple of chocolate assortments received as Christmas gifts completed the candy section. My most involved dessert would be the apple pie, golden and crisp, another favorite of the younger niece.

I headed off to the store on the Thursday before Christmas with a sense of dread. A giant snowstorm, dubbed the "Holiday Blizzard" by our (not so) imaginative area newscasters, dropped upwards of 36 inches of snow on the closest city, leaving the grocery trucks stranded and our grocery shelves increasingly empty as the weekend moved on. I escaped from my office with the first story of empty shelves and joined a panicked pack of shoppers at the store. Along with everyone else, I pared down and amended and re-planned my menus, but had arrived early enough that I didn't have to do much with anything but side dishes. The one big sacrifice was a decrease in the amount of eggnog when I saw the bare ten dozen eggs remaining on the shelves. I opted only for one dozen, with the thought of finding more at the health food store (a required stop anyway for the ground elk I was substituting in the shepherds pie). I even found a beautiful frenched rack of lamb for our elegant Christmas dinner, along with fresh rosemary for the sauce, yams for roasting and fresh green beans for our sides. I happily scouted out a couple of exotic cheeses and made a quick visit to my favorite wine and gourmet food shop before heading back to the house to store my gigantic sack of goodies.

Then came the news. The nieces, delayed by the Holiday Blizzard, had been bumped from yet another flight and now were delayed until the twenty-eighth. Their heartbroken mother called with the news right after Auntie Honey-Bunny got off the telephone with her sobbing nieces. We soothed as best we could and looked at each other with philosophical sighs. A quick sob caught in my throat. How would we eat all of this food?

Re-plan, re-strategize, and re-stock. A few quick calculations and I was off to the races. New plans for leftover ham and a delayed but still delicious apple pie filled my head like sugarplum dreams. The gigantic shepherd's pie wouldn't wait (I could only rearrange so much without confronting the empty stores again), but that made excellent leftovers for another supper and two lunches during the next week. The next Thursday shopping run was sparse, but finally yielded the evasive lentils for the soup – something I had pared away the week before.

And the nieces finally arrived despite the second blizzard threatening my, I mean their (!), plans.

Amazing brunches and suppers awaited them, along with a Christmas dessert table to please any proud housewyfe. A tall poinsettia, golden wire reindeer and candles set serenely on a flat sheet of mirror created a beautiful backdrop for the cake pedestal, surrounded by plates of cookies and candy. My special Christmas dessert plates completed the abundant table, and I felt like the consummate hostess: menu plans in place, Christmas music on my stereo and a glass of sparkling wine in my hand.

Remember Lesbian Law #1:

"Never Underestimate the Power of a Lesbian Housewyfe."

I think it's time for that bottle of wine.

MULLED CIDER

As fall gallops forward into winter, and the holidays descend upon us like a pack of starving dogs, I like to keep mulled cider around. This concoction comes together quickly, and stores nicely for easy reheating when unexpected guests arrive to deliver packages or simply to hang out and hide from their sweet, well-intentioned, but utterly misguided families.

1 gallon apple cider
1 cup orange juice
1 orange, sliced thinly

1 lemon, sliced thinly
1" ginger root, sliced thinly
2 sticks cinnamon
1 shake or two grinds nutmeg
1 teaspoon whole cloves

Mix together in a crock pot. Heat on high until hot. Allow the brew to simmer for 10 minutes and then remove the orange, lemon, ginger root, cinnamon and cloves. I use one of those shallow strainers that you see so often in Asian cooking. Enjoy it right away or let mellow on low for several hours while the flavors blend. This brew lasts for quite a few days if kept refrigerated.

·❤·❤·❤·❤·❤·

As the Snow Blows

A whirring noise wakes me. A bleary blinking eye turns toward the window and sees the telltale spout of snow blowing straight up into the air from the sound in his driveway. Able to see only my neighbor, barely recognizable in his swaddled warmness, over the tall bank of snow, the noise and spray of snow have given him away. He's playing with his snowblower.

My sweet honey bunny is always quick to regale me with tales of our wonderful snowblower. This giant monster begins with a quick electric start, warming the handles and igniting the headlight to reveal what the giant maw of gyrating teeth will destroy.

"See how easy?" She crows in triumph as she simply pushes the button to start the motor. She really, really loves to snowblow. "Anyone can do it." She looks at me meaningfully.

I glance down and away like a child avoiding the knowledge that their mother, staring straight down at them and saying "isn't it nice to have a clean room?" wants them to clean their room. I give her an encouraging smile, so hopefully she will think that I was not avoiding the subject. "That's great, honey. I really do like the snowblower. It makes your job so much easier."

A volley bounces the ball back into her court.

"Let me show you how to use it."

Her return lobs the ball up and over my head, landing with a distinct POP just inside the line.

My sweet honey bunny circles the snowblower, moving a couple of levers and unhooking the electric cord to move it out of the way now that the snowblower is running. I watch her mysterious movements like I will remember them. I seem to be incapable of remembering how to run this machine. Perhaps I should go get my notebook.

She's progressing, giving me instructions like I will retain any of her words.

"The right handle makes the machine go forward and the left starts the big teeth."

I think this is what she said. Argh. I should have gotten my notebook.

"Here are the gears..."

Gears? Like in a car? Doesn't this thing just have a big D?

"And here's the knob to move the chute. Turn it left for the snow to go right and right for it to go left."

What? Okay. Opposite world. I'm sure I'll get this.

"Now, the turtle means that the machine will go slower and the rabbit means faster."

Isn't this opposite world? I'm confused again.

Do I say any of these things? No! I simply smile and nod like I understand. I've picked up many more complex things than this just by looking and trying it out.

"Okay. Just go for it."

I grab both handles and push down. The machine immediately jumps and spins and shoots forward. I simply hold on and wonder how I'm going to avoid hitting the recycling bins. I'm not. I'm going to smash into them and grind them to pieces and they will be destroyed and we will have to go beg some more from the garbage company and they will laugh and laugh and laugh when they find out how this happened.

"Just let go! Just let go!" I hear through the cloud of panic in my mind. Somehow, I make my hands understand that by releasing, the giant monster will stop. The machine stops moving.

"I'll finish it." My sweet honey bunny looks at me with dismay. "Just go inside."

I've disappointed her once again.

And I'm not appropriately sorry about it.

The snowblower scares me. That giant maw of spinning sharp edges startles me each time it starts. The same feeling looms when I help with power tools. Those saws could really hurt you, and I'm appropriately afraid. The only other thing that gets me like this is a gun. Guns hold the same terror for me. Simply seeing one in someone's hand starts the butterflies flipping around my stomach and I feel a scrunching squeeze on my heart that grabs my throat and stops my breathing.

Yep. I'm definitely afraid of inanimate objects with sharp edges and/or pointy edges and/or exploding bits. There's no getting around it.

I used to think that if I learned how to use them, I could control my fear. I worked in the shop at the theater department when I was in college and immediately volunteered to use the large sharp power saw. Using the equipment would overcome my fear!

Following my quick raised hand and a tour of the shop, I was treated to a litany of all of the ways that the saw could hurt me. With visions of dismembered digits and limbs, I quickly de-volunteered to use the saw and went to find a hammer. The shop director stopped me.

"You're really afraid of these things?" He said, gesturing to the large table saw and crosscut saw behind him.

"Please. I'll just hammer something. I'll be fine. I don't have to learn how to use them."

Wrong answer. This answer actually means "I have a healthy fear of these objects and will treat them with the respect and wariness they deserve. I will never hurt myself on them because I am so scared of losing a digit that I will always take the proper safety precautions."

Dang it!

Power tool duty for four years of theater shop. And I came out just as scared as when I went in. This should have taught me that actually becoming proficient on these tools wouldn't make a difference in my alert level, but it didn't.

A mere ten years later, I found myself standing on a gun range, pointing a .22 handgun at a target with a man who thought I was learning how to protect myself. I, of course, was at alert level "orange."

"Just pull gently on the trigger."

Pop! The bullet exited the barrel and slammed into the target. Immediately, I removed my finger from the trigger and stuck it out longways along the trigger guard. I lowered the gun to my side. Frankly, I'd expected more to happen. Some sort of big jerk or sound or backlash from the force expanding from the barrel.

"Nice." The fellow smiled. "Look. You hit the target."

I squinted and saw the small hole between the largest dot in the center and the next ring out. Not bad. I almost felt proud. Then, I turned to my helpful new friend who smiled until he saw that I'd raised the gun inadvertently.

"Make sure to always point a loaded gun at the ground, even if the safety is on." He pushed my hand down and smiled with panic filling his eyes. "Don't want to shoot anyone by accident." Chuckling, he continued. "How about another shot?"

Not wanting to seem embarrassed by almost killing him, I nodded and finished out the bullets loaded into the gun.

Afterwards, driving away from the gun range, I felt powerful. I had no idea that with so little force, I could kill something. I could protect myself. I'd overcome my fear. I patted the gun training manuals we'd been handed at the end of our class. I could get a concealed weapons license. All things were possible.

Then I shook my head. I could also see the possibilities. There I am at Safeway with my gun safely stored in my purse. As I push myself through the crowded aisles, I accidentally grab my pistol instead of my shopping list. The next thing I know, I have to pay not only for a new tile in the floor, but an entire line of boxes of Cheerios and a new purse. Who knows how long the rampage would continue until the gun jammed because my shopping list got caught in the action? My shooting instructor warned us about keeping semi-automatic weapons in our purses for just that reason!

And how would I explain the situation to the police? You know someone would call the police. People really tend to be unforgiving in these sorts of situations.

"But Officer, I didn't mean to fire the gun. I was grabbing my shopping list and the gun got in the way and I grabbed it instead and accidentally disengaged the safety with my pinky and then the gun just started going off because my lipstick got caught in the little trigger space, but then the shopping list got caught in the action and jammed it. Isn't that lucky? Really?"

I can only imagine the icy stoniness of the look in the police officer's eyes as he insists on arresting me. Even if I managed to not harm anyone, I can't imagine that he'd only give me a ticket and send me home.

And Safeway would definitely ban me for life.

Yep. Understanding the possibilities and a healthy imagination have always fueled my fear of these deadly objects. I just can't turn off my mind.

So, when confronted by the not-so-sophisticated machine outside my front door, I freeze. Who knows what havoc I could wreak with such a large pointy object? The wheels alone mean that I could accidentally go on a rampage.

I know. I shouldn't underestimate myself. After all, I know Lesbian Law #1: Never Underestimate the Power of a Lesbian Housewyfe.

Besides, I could end up with snowblower duty for the rest of my life.

Acknowledgements

First, I have to thank YOU.

Yep. You.

Thank you for reading this book, for supporting my writing, and for sharing my words with your friends and family. I wouldn't be able to do what I do without that support.

Specifically...

Thank you to the ladies of the Mud Season Writer's Group: Joanne Palmer, Jill Murphy-Long, Deb Funston, Elizabeth Bartasius, LuEtta Loeber, Susana Field, and Kate Krautkramer. Your edits and tips are found throughout this book, and made it readable for the rest of us.

Thank you to Kathryn Gray. Girlfriend. Your unconditional love and support has gotten me through patches so rough the road felt like it was one big pothole. And that's no joke.

Thanks to Janet Selbe and Nancy Paul for sending me love, laughter, and the occasional check at exactly the right time.

Thank you to everyone who showed up and supported me through BuyMeACoffee.com and Substack. Your cups of tea kept me awake and writing through the darkest hours, and the subscriptions allow me to share my silly on a regular basis.

Thanks to my entire family for laughing with me as I share our stories with the world. These tales come from the tangled strands of Bourgeois, Baldwin, Bruner, and Reineke. I hope you share my delight at these silly words.

(And thank you for your concern but no. Neither of us use our mother's maiden name for ANY of our password security.)

Finally, thank you to my wyfe, Stephanie. Your unconditional love and support helped me make this jump into writing full-time. What a crazy life we've led, my love! I'm looking forward to many more years with you.

·❤·❤·❤·❤·❤·

A Final Introduction

For those of you who don't know me, I'm LA (as in tra-la-la) Bourgeois, the Lesbian Housewyfe.

While I aspire to be kind, I consider "nice" an annoying personality quirk. I'm that friend who drops by for a chit-chat and makes you spit your tea all over your new tablecloth.

Want more giggles? Follow the Lesbian Housewyfe's journey in her weekly missive filled with funny stories of modern living interspersed with household tips. And a little knitting. And tons about the pets because, you know, lesbians and their pets!

Visit Housewyfe.com and sign up for the newsletter to get new essays each week.

I'll see you there!

ABOUT THE AUTHOR

LA Bourgeois experimented with many identities before accepting that she was a Writer. She fled from Arkansas to Colorado upon graduating from high school. After receiving her B.A. in English with an emphasis in Drama from the University of Denver in 1992, she married her wife, Stephanie, and began her journey as the Lesbian House-wyfe. Gardening, cooking, crafting, and writing about her ridiculous approach to life became her passion. She moved to Steamboat Springs in 1997, where she embraced entrepreneurship and ran various businesses including an internet service provider, cafe, and liquor store. But also, she picked up knitting needles and became a knitting professional, designing and tech-editing knitting patterns, teaching knitting, and partnering with a group of ladies to run a yarn and fabric shop. In 2022, she became a Kaizen-Muse Certified Creativity Coach to empower people to manifest their creative dreams. You can find her writing in publications such as Psychology Today, Writer's Fun Zone, Beyondish, and the Ithaca Times. She lives in Ithaca, NY with her wife, sister-in-law, a primary-school friend of theirs, and Mack the Dog.

www.ingramcontent.com/pod-product-compliance
Lightning Source LLC
Chambersburg PA
CBHW020159090426
42734CB00008B/880

* 9 7 9 8 9 9 0 1 7 6 8 1 2 *